Whiskers and Tales

# Whiskers and Tales

*Service Dogs, Family Pets, and Animal Shelters*

A collection of essays by Jill D. Sweet

Animal Portraits by Mary Jane Kotsi

*Jill Sweet*
*+ moses*

The Troy Book Makers, Troy NY

Whiskers and Tales: Service Dogs, Family Pets, and Animal Shelters

Copyright © 2012 by Jill D. Sweet

All rights Reserved. No part of this book may be used or reproduced in any manner whatsoever without written permission from the author except in the case of brief quotations embodied in critical articles and reviews.

To order additional copies of this title, contact your favorite local bookstore or visit www.tbmbooks.com

Cover and book design by Linda D. Wilkes

Copy editing by Anne K. Proulx

Cover images: www.istockphoto.com/stefan1234

www.istockphoto.com/HannamariaH

Author photo by Mark Bolles,
Creative Photo and Graphic

Printed in the United States of America

The Troy Book Makers

www.thetroybookmakers.com

ISBN: 978-1-61468-102-1

*For Moses' puppy raiser, Bethany Koetje*

Proceeds from the sale of this book will benefit

Friends of the Saratoga County Animal Shelter,
Homes for Orphaned Pets Exist (H.O.P.E.)
and The Estherville Animal Sanctuary.

# Contents

Introduction to Whiskers & Tales, The Book ........................ 1

Animals & Disabilities   (March 6, 2009) ........................ 3

Growing a Relationship Between Cats & Dogs   (March 13, 2009)... 4

Caring for Rabbits   (March 20, 2009) ........................... 6

Dealing With Pet Obesity   (March 27, 2009)..................... 8

Surrendered Pets   (April 3, 2009)............................. 10

Adoption of Older & Special Needs Animals   (April 10, 2009).... 12

An Everyday "Hero," Daisy Mae's Tiny Tale   (April 10, 2009) ...... 16

Pit Bulls: Vicious or Beloved, but Misunderstood?   (April 17, 2009) 16

Three Families & Their Adopted Shelter Pets   (April 24, 2009) .... 19

Children & Dog Bites   (May 1, 2009) .......................... 23

It's All About The Animals   (May 8, 2009) ..................... 25

Max, Vida, & Sully   (May 15, 2009)........................... 28

Beau & Bella, Two Maine Coon Cats   (May 29, 2009) ............ 30

Follow-Up On Three Pet Stories   (May 29, 2009) ................ 32

Summertime, When The Liv'in Is Easy   (June 5, 2009) ........... 35

Presidents & First Dogs   (June 12, 2009)....................... 40

Parakeets or Budgies— Little Social Birds   (June 26, 2009) ...... 42

Hap's Story   (July 3, 2009).................................... 45

Please Leave The Wildlife Alone!!!   (July 17, 2009)............... 49

H.O.P.E., Friends, & the Saratoga
County Animal Shelter   (July 24, 2009) ....................... 52

My Dog Vida & Her Sixth Sense?   (July 31, 2009)................ 54

Sully the Cat Speaks Out   (Aug. 14, 2009) ..................... 56

Lions & Tigers & Bears, Oh My!   (Aug. 21, 2009) ................ 59

More on Cats   (Aug. 28, 2009)................................ 61

The Overpopulated World of Pets   (Sept. 4, 2009) ............... 63

The Healing Power of Dogs   (Sept. 11, 2009) .................... 66

Estherville, A Family Run Animal Sanctuary   (Sept. 25, 2009) ..... 68

A Good Dog Is A Trained Dog   (Oct. 2, 2009).................... 71

Ling, the Chinese Dwarf Hamster   (Oct. 23, 2009) ............... 73

Canine Companions for Independence   (Oct. 30, 2009).......... 74

My CCI Class   (Nov. 20, 2009) ................................. 76

Moses & Our Pack   (Nov. 25, 2009) ........................... 80

Training at Canine Companions for Independence   (Dec. 4, 2009) . 82

Puppy Raisers, Unsung Heroes In the
Making of an Assistance Dog   (Dec. 11, 2009) .................. 84

Happy Holidays, But Remember Dangers for Pets   (Dec. 18, 2009) 87

Pets & Heroic Acts   (Dec. 24, 2009)............................ 89

New Year's Resolutions for You & Your Pet   (Jan. 8, 2010) ........ 92

How Cold is Too Cold to Walk the Dog?   (Jan. 22, 2010).......... 94

Dementia in Dogs & Cats   (Jan. 29, 2010)....................... 96

Oh My Aching Back! Arthritis In Older Dogs & Cats   (Feb. 5, 2010) . 99

Hyperthyroidism, Hypertension, & Heart Disease   (Feb. 12, 2010) 101

Establishing a Strong Bond Between You
& Your Pet: The Importance of Regular Grooming   (Feb. 19, 2010) 103

The World According to Moses   (Feb. 26, 2010) ................ 105

Pets, Boredom & Cabin Fever   (March 5, 2010) ................ 107

I Know I Am Not Supposed To Pet, But . . .   (March 12, 2010) .... 110

Animal Cruelty, Neglect & Abuse   (March 19, 2010) ............ 112

Suspecting & Reporting Animal
Abuse in Your Community   (March 26, 2010) .................. 114

The Black Magic Cat   (April 1, 2010)........................... 117

An Extraordinary Book About An
Extraordinary Dog   (April 9, 2010)............................ 119

Disruption In the Pack   (April 30, 2010)........................ 121

Reuniting the Pack & Other Matters   (May 7, 2010) ............. 123

Mosey's First Ride on an Airplane   (May 14, 2010) ............... 125

Swimming Dogs  (May 21, 2010).............................127

Springtime, Finally!  (May 27, 2010)...........................129

Pets as Antidepressants & Pets as Obsessions  (May 28, 2010)...131

What It Takes To Make a Service Dog  (June 4, 2010)...........133

Holistic Veterinarian Medicine  (June 18, 2010)................136

The Joy of Adopting an Older Cat  (July 2, 2010)...............138

Year of the Fish & the Age of Aquariums  (July 9, 2010).........140

Vida & Old Age  (July 23, 2010)...............................142

Search & Rescue Dogs  (July 30, 2010).........................144

Feral Cats & Kittens  (Aug. 6, 2010)...........................146

Keeping a Trained Dog Trained
(Keeping a Good Dog Good)  (Aug. 13, 2010)...................149

Is the Saratoga County Shelter
A "No-Kill" Shelter?  (Sept. 17, 2010)..........................151

Friends Benefit  (Oct. 29, 2010)...............................153

Grand Opening of the New County Shelter  (Nov. 12, 2010)......155

Boo & Pets That Escape  (Nov. 24, 2010)......................157

Pets & the Upcoming Holidays  (Dec. 17, 2010).................159

Two Pet Peeves at the Spa State Park  (Jan. 7, 2011)............161

In Memory of Vida (1998-2011)  (Feb. 4, 2011)..................164

Greyhounds & Dog Racing  (March 18 2011)...................167

Traveling to New Hampshire With Moses  (April 29, 2011)......169

Blessing of the Animals  (July 22, 2011).......................172

Winning Over Joan  (Aug. 12, 2011)...........................175

Humans Aiding Animals,
Animals Aiding Humans, Part I  (Aug. 26, 2011)................178

Humans Aiding Animals, Animals
Aiding Humans, Part II  (Sept. 2, 2011).......................180

A Two-Week Road Trip
(From a Lab's Point of View)  (Nov. 11, 2011)..................182

The Road Trip, Part II   (Nov. 18, 2011) . . . . . . . . . . . . . . . . . . . . . . . . 185
The Holidays & A New Family Pet   (Dec. 16, 2011) . . . . . . . . . . . . . . 188
Jessie Finds Her Forever Home   (Jan. 13, 2012) . . . . . . . . . . . . . . . . 190
Closing   . . . . . . . . . . . . . . . . . . . . . . . . . . . . . . . . . . . . . . . . . . . . . . . . . . 193

# Introduction to Whiskers and Tales, The Book

This book is a collection of short essays that first appeared as columns on the Pet Page of *Saratoga Today*, a weekly newspaper read by many residents of Saratoga Springs, New York. The column, "Whiskers and Tales," featured a wide range of topics such as service dogs, feral cats, puppy mills, illegal exotic pets, animal training, care, and health. Some of the stories are told from my point of view and others are told from my animals' points of view. Some subject matter, like animal hoarding, neglect, or abuse might make readers shed a tear while others might make them smile or even laugh.

The stories are presented here in the order they appeared in the newspaper. This order reveals how over time I became more comfortable writing the column. Soon I began to introduce and share anecdotes about my family of pets. The stories developed into a combination of important information for pet owners, alongside personal revelations and some flights of fantasy such as a sassy cat speaking his mind about canines or a service dog describing a face-to-face encounter with a five-point buck.

These stories were written for all ages. Many are even appropriate for parents to read aloud to their young children. After all, it is never too early to inspire children to love, respect and care for animals. Three themes that run through many of the stories include, (1) humans helping animals, (2) animals helping humans, and (3) the importance of spay/neuter as a responsible and humane way to curtail pet overpopulation. There simply are too many animals and too few "forever homes" for them.

To update the stories, there have been a couple of developments that deserve comment. First, Friends of the Saratoga County Animal Shelter (FSCAS) have reached their goal of helping the county shelter transition from the old to the new facility. FSCAS have also let the county residents know that the new shelter is a beautiful state-of-the-art establishment open for adoptions, surrenders, volunteerism, and education. In addition, FSCAS have established a fund for shelter animal medical costs not covered by the county. With these central goals met, the board of FSCAS voted to shift the non-profit into a period of dormancy, until the need again arises for a more active organization. Second, Homes for Orphaned Pets (H.O.P.E.) has opened a low-cost spay/neuter clinic just outside of Saratoga Springs in Wilton, New York. This clinic has made spay/neuter affordable and can only help in the fight against pet overpopulation that leads to neglected animals and euthanasia. Third, Estherville has established regular fundraising events and recently received a donated new van for transporting animals, employees, and volunteers.

Sales of these books will go to benefit these three local organizations. All of them have volunteers who work tirelessly for homeless pets in our community. Further, thanks are due to designer Linda Wilkes and editor Anne Proulx, as well as donors Michelle Dudley, Sandy Zanone, and Pat Casey, as well as the Troy Bookmakers for helping to make Whiskers and Tales, the book, a reality.

Sincerely,

Jill D. Sweet

## Animals and Disabilities
(March 6, 2009)

Animals can make all the difference for an individual living with a disability. There are certified trained service dogs that guide the blind, bring out-of-reach objects to individuals in wheelchairs, and some intuitive service dogs can detect and warn an epileptic of a seizure, minutes before it actually occurs. But even pets without special training can help individuals suffering from conditions such as depression, dementia, multiple sclerosis, cancer, stroke, heart disease, and other debilitating circumstances.

Martha, who suffers from multiple sclerosis, depression and anxiety, reports that "just brushing or petting my cat, Jingles, calms me and seems to take away my stress and my worries about the future. Jingles takes my mind off my problems, at least for awhile." Actually scientists have found that handling pets can lower one's blood pressure.

Pets are also important because they have needs. They must be fed, groomed and in the case of dogs, they need to be walked. This makes pets a way for the owner to get out in the fresh air and meet people. Mark, who is a stroke survivor says his dog, Rex, gets him out and meeting people even with his speech, which was impacted by the stoke. Mark explains, "My dog makes it easier to talk to people. They focus on Rex rather than my difficulties with words."

In addition, pets are helpful in that they expect a routine. They are creatures of habit. They know when it is time to eat and when it is time to sleep. As a result, they can be a predictable feature in their owner's life, when so much else has become topsy-turvy with the disruption of an illness. Further, any pet owner will tell you that his or her pet makes a great listener, one who doesn't judge and asks for little more than food, warmth, and some play and affection in return.

Today, the better nursing homes are aware of the benefits of having visiting and resident animals on the premises. Some floors have a cat that is free to roam and others welcome regular visits from licensed therapy dogs. Many of the elderly miss having a cat or dog of their own, and when they can hold or see animals in the nursing home, they can reminisce about a lifetime of animals they once loved and for which they dearly cared. When Douglas' father was seriously ill in a nursing home, the resident cat would not leave his side until he passed. Apparently this was not the first time this same cat was drawn to the side of a dying resident.

## Growing a Relationship Between Cats and Dogs
(March 13, 2009)

Sometimes people come to the Saratoga County Animal Shelter looking to adopt a cat but are hesitant because they already have a dog. Other times it is just the opposite; they want to bring home a dog, but they already have a cat. The phrase, "they fought like cats and dogs" must have come from some reality in the domestic animal world. Nevertheless, there are millions of people who do not consider the family complete without a dog and a cat. Wasn't that the model in the early Dick and Jane books? Wasn't there a cat named Puff and a dog named Spot?

Dogs and cats can co-exist, especially when they grow up together. The optimal time to introduce a cat and a dog is when the dog is less than one year and the cat is less than six months. Things can get a little bit more difficult, however, when one or the other is older and already well established in the home. But with patience and some training, older cats and dogs can learn at least to tolerate each other. Two years ago, I brought home a shelter kitten named Sully to meet my eleven-year-old black lab, Vida, and soon after they were curling up together for naps on Vida's dog bed.

Both cats and dogs are predators. Dogs typically chase their prey and cats usually pounce on their victims. Both will bite and shake the animal until it is too wounded to survive. Typically cats are graceful and almost playful in their deadly pursuits. In comparison, dogs can be clumsy and reckless but they get the job done just the same. Because dogs are usually larger than cats they have an advantage (my friend's Maine Coon cat that tips the scales at 18 lbs. is an exception).

Dogs are the ones that need to be trained to never chase or harm cats. Why is it the dog that needs to learn the rules? Well, if you have ever tried to teach your cat to respond to specific commands, you know that they usually look at you like you are nuts and they go about their independent lives as they see fit. Dogs, on the other hand, are much more eager to please. My dog will learn just about anything for a biscuit and some praise whereas my cat cooperates with my requests only when it is convenient. The difference is one reason why many people want both a cat and a dog. They love the obedience and loyalty of a dog and the independence of a cat.

The keys for training dogs to respect cats rather than chase them include the commands sit/stay, down/stay and leave it. Begin the training with your dog wearing a training collar and a leash. Put the dog in a sit/stay or down/stay while a friend holds the cat at the other side of the room. Your dog might whine or get excited at smelling and seeing the cat, but insist he remain in the sit or down/stay. Praise him when he cooperates. At first keep the sessions short, gradually lengthening them. At each session bring the cat closer. If your dog lunges toward the cat give him a sharp correction with the leash and say "LEAVE IT!" Be firm, but never lose your temper. To quote TV sensation, Cesar Millan (the dog whisperer), "always be calm and assertive."

As your dog becomes more reliable, you can let him approach the cat and eventually you can take off the leash. You should always supervise these early interactions. It is also important that the cat has some place to get away from the dog. These free zones can be a room with a gate that only the cat can get through or a high perch that only the cat can climb. How long will it take to train your dog to refrain from chasing your cat depends on his "prey drive" or the intensity of his instinct to chase and catch prey. Scent and the movement of another animal will trigger a dog's prey drive. The ultimate test of control for your dog is to stay down and be calm even when the cat runs past. If these efforts to train your dog do not succeed, you may have to resort to simply keeping the dog and cat separated in the house. This will be particularly important during meal times when animals can become aggressively protective about their food.

## Caring for Rabbits
(March 20, 2009)

Easter is near and that means Easter bonnets, Easter lilies, and Easter bunnies. There are chocolate bunnies, plush stuffed-animal bunnies, and unfortunately for the animals, there are living breathing bunnies given as Easter gifts to young children for their short-term entertainment. Too often children handle these live baby rabbits roughly and as soon as the novelty wears off, they are "set free" only to become easy prey to hawks, foxes, coyotes, and domestic cats or dogs. While only a little better than simply letting them loose in an open field to become "food," domestic rabbits also end up in animal shelters after the Easter celebrations are over. The worst part of this situation is that the children involved come away with the idea that pets are disposable, and it is OK to toss them aside when the newness wears off.

Don't misunderstand, rabbits can be wonderful pets, but people need to understand that caring for them properly takes time, money, and work. Bunnies quickly grow up to be rabbits that can live for ten or more years. During their life span there will be occasions when they need medical care. Veterinarians skilled in rabbit health can be expensive and hard to find. Further, rabbits need a clean dry place to live with fresh water and washed fresh greens daily. With adult supervision, taking care of a rabbit can be a great opportunity for older children to learn about the responsibilities of animal care. The experience of caring for a rabbit properly can help them see their pets as much more than throwaways.

The House Rabbit Society, www.rabbit.org, is a humane nonprofit rescue and education organization that reports every year a huge increase in the number of abandoned rabbits after Easter. They argue that rabbits are not low maintenance pets and are a poor choice for young children. They claim that domestic rabbits should not live alone in a hutch outdoors, but rather they are very social animals that enjoy gentle human interaction. They explain that rabbits are meticulously clean animals that easily learn to use a kitty litter box and can live inside the home, at least part of the time. Finally, the organization recommends pet rabbits be neutered or spayed because unaltered rabbits will exhibit territorial behavior such as boxing, nipping, or spraying, and the females are more likely to develop uterine cancer.

So please, this Easter think twice about impulsively buying a living bunny for a child. A chocolate bunny is a better choice. And if it is something cuddly you want to give, stay with the stuffed-animal type of bunny. At the moment, there are two beautiful grown rabbits at the Saratoga County Animal Shelter where they wait for a new caring family to adopt them. Sadly, however, you can bet there will be more rabbits waiting there soon after Easter is past.

## Dealing With Pet Obesity
(March 27, 2009)

As the leaves begin to turn and the mornings become chilly, I am reminded that before long it will be winter. With winter comes less activity for humans and pets. With less activity we all are more likely to put on a few extra pounds.

It always makes me sad when I see a very overweight dog or cat lumbering along with labored breathing. I feel badly for them because, with few exceptions, their obesity is the direct result of their owner's failure to give them regular exercise, and at the same time, overfeeding them. Too much dog or cat food, endless table scraps, and pet treats with little or no exercise can only lead to weight gain. Just like with people, an overweight pet faces many illnesses related to obesity such as diabetes, arthritis, and joint pain. Actually, carrying excess weight puts greater demands on every organ of the body. The heart, the muscles, the ligaments, the circulation system and the respiratory system all can be harmed. Overweight animals have less endurance and less stamina. If your pet is overweight, her life expectancy will be at least 15% shorter than if she is fit and trim.

Interestingly, as the average weight of American children and adults has risen, so has the average weight of American pets. In each case, there has been a drop in activity and an increase in caloric intake. Children aren't riding their bikes as much, adults are not walking as much, and no one seems to have time to play string games with the cat or fetch with the dog. As a cat gets older he needs to be inspired to play. For a dog, the walk is essential throughout her life. Even if you have a fenced-in yard dogs need the structure of a walk with a family member. If your dog pulls on walks, making it an unpleasant or even a dangerous experience, it may be time for an obedience course or for a refresher class.

According to the Association for Pet Obesity Prevention (APOP), over 44% of dogs and 57% of cats are considered overweight or obese. APOP, an organization of veterinarians dedicated to reducing pet obesity, claims that obesity is the leading cause of preventable diseases and death in cats and dogs. These veterinarians point out that a few extra pounds on a small dog or cat is the equivalent to 30-50 extra pounds on a human. To learn more about this professional organization and the studies they have conducted, visit www.petobesityprevention.com.

In an effort to not overfeed your pet, follow the recommended portions on the package, taking into account your pet's age and weight. It is also a good idea to measure the food. If you decide to change your pet's food from one type to another, always make the change gradually. Sudden changes in diet can upset your pet's digestive system. In terms of treats for dogs, some like small pieces of crunchy apples or carrots. You can also purchase very small dog biscuits to occasionally reward good behavior. If you can't resist your dog's sorrowful eyes or her begging antics, put her outside or in another room while you are eating.

Of course overeating is not always the owner's doing. Some breeds and some individual dogs are relentless "chow hounds." My black lab, Vida has always eaten her food so quickly, people think I have been starving her. In her dog training classes, her teacher, Michelle Dudley always said Vida was a food-driven dog that would do anything for a biscuit. My most enthusiastic eater, however, was my Beagle, Boo, who ate an entire turkey carcass one Thanksgiving. She pulled it from the garbage and before I realized it, Boo ate every bone of that bird, lay on her back for a time with an enormous extended stomach, but never even got sick! My vet was amazed.

In this society we often equate love and food. But if your pet is overweight, you may need to show your love and affection with a tummy rub, a scratch behind the ears, a walk, or a game of catch, rather than with a big slice of your dinner pot roast. After all, if food is the only way you feel you can love them, you may just end up literally killing them with your misplaced love.

Pet Tip— Warning signs of Pet Diabetes

- Your pet is drinking more water and urinating more frequently
- Your pet suddenly begins to lose weight
- Your pet suddenly has cataract formations
- Your pet is dehydrated

## Surrendered Pets
(April 3, 2009)

Most animals that end up in our county animal shelter are labeled either "surrenders" or "strays." The latter category refers to lost or abandoned animals that are saved by the county animal control officers. Some of the lost animals are claimed and happily reunited with their owners, while others are never claimed and after a period of time, become candidates for adoption. But what about the first category, "surrenders?" What does it mean for a pet to be surrendered and why does it happen?

Owners give up or surrender their pets to the shelter for a variety of reasons. Sometimes the stated reason is a family member develops allergies. Other reasons given include the owner's death, military deployment, or the need to move to an apartment that does not allow pets. The most common reason stated, however, is simply "the owner can no longer care for the animal." When I go through the list of animals up for adoption on the county shelter web site and I read that statement, I can't help but wonder about the circumstances.

Perhaps the reason is an economic one. In an economic recession (or depression, depending on which expert you believe), where people are losing their homes, their jobs, or their retirement savings, a pet might be seen as just one more drain on the family budget, especially if that pet needs veterinary care. My heart goes out to individuals who have to choose between caring for their dog or cat and paying next month's rent. Several groups, including the Friends of the Saratoga County Animal Shelter, have started pet food drives with the hopes that if food banks can offer pet food along with groceries for feeding the family, fewer people will have to give up their pets.

Another possible scenario involves the young couple that adopts a dog as a test case before bringing a baby into their lives. Sadly for the dog, after the couple decides to have a baby, and nine months later when they bring the newborn home, suddenly there is no time or energy for the dog. The couple may even fear the dog could harm the baby. As kids, many of us remember Disney's Lady and the Tramp where the cocker spaniel, Lady, is warned by the stray, Tramp, that once the baby comes home, she will be homeless just like him. Of course this is Disney animation and in the end, not only is Lady able to stay in her home along with the baby, the couple adopts Tramp as well. I think they even take in a litter of Lady and Tramp's puppies! Not very likely in the real world.

Another set of circumstances might involve a divorce. Perhaps neither partner wants the responsibility of a dog or cat as they struggle to start a new life. Giving up a pet might also be necessary when the owner faces a long-term rehabilitation after surgery. Sometimes college students will surrender their cat or dog after graduation. Yet another reason animals are taken to the shelter occurs when an unaltered pet becomes pregnant and gives birth "so the children in the family can experience the miracle of life." After all the excitement is over, however, not all the offspring find homes and the "leftovers" are dropped off at the shelter. Older dogs and cats that have been surrendered are less likely to be adopted than the kittens and puppies. Their situation is particularly poignant; after years of loyalty, they suddenly find themselves in a strange new environment filled with unfamiliar scents, sounds and faces.

There are many reasons for dogs and cats to be surrendered at the shelter, and none of them are the fault of the animal. Even if a dog is surrendered because it is aggressive, because it is a constant barker, or because it is a digger, more likely than not, these unwanted behaviors are the result of a dog that is bored, neglected, mistreated, under exercised or under trained. Further, if a cat is surrendered because he suddenly stops using his kitty litter box, this can be the result of a big change in the household and the stress that it can cause for the animal. A cat can even stop using the box because his owner is neglecting to change the kitty litter regularly.

## Adoption of Older and Special Needs Animals
(April 10, 2009)

When older animals or animals with special needs end up in our county animal shelter, it takes some very special and caring individuals to take them in and give them a forever home. Last week in my column on surrendered pets,

I referred to the challenge of finding homes for older pets that, for a myriad of reasons, are left at the shelter. Take for example shelter cats Buddy, Marie, and Ramesea, who are all eight years old. As it is soon to be the season for kittens, these older cats will be passed over for the little ones. The adult cats may have served their owners well over the years, but suddenly they find themselves in need of a quiet, secure and loving home.

While most people who come to the shelter looking to adopt a pet never take the older ones, senior cats are just the type of animals that Angel and Joe Maenhardt will seriously consider bringing home. Why do they do this? What are the rewards and what are the emotional and economic costs? I talked with this exceptional couple and learned that while adopting the older and special needs cats is not for everyone, for those who do adopt them, the rewards can make it all worthwhile. What Angel and Joe do is very much like hospice for orphaned pets.

## Q & A

*Jill interviews Angel and Joe*

*J:* Why do you adopt older and special needs animals from the shelter?

*Angel:* They are the overlooked ones. The younger healthier animals are always put forward. When we first see these older animals, we look at them with our hearts, not our eyes. We feel their fear and confusion, and we know we can help them through the final days, months, or even years of their lives.

Our county shelter is more humane than most. They give the older ones a second or even a third, fourth, or fifth chance at being adopted. They even provide cats for a "senior to senior" program sponsored by the Office of the Aging, where more mature cats are paired with senior citizens. It has been a very successful program.

*Joe:* Angel and I have been adopting older cats for fifteen years now. If there are medical expenses, we simply do what we can do to make the animal comfortable. Sometimes it is only to get some antibiotics for a urinary tract infection, other times it is simply finding a vet to pull a painful tooth. But we don't feel we must go to extreme measures or to very expensive remedies to help the animal. After all, this is an older animal we brought into our home from the typically stressful shelter environment—when no one else came forward. So we do what we can do, and we do it within our means.

*Angel:* Sometimes we look to vitamin therapy or alternative medicine and other times we use discount animal supplies from sources like the Foster and Grant catalogue, where medicines can be less expensive.

*Joe:* While we care deeply about these animals, we do not let them keep us from our love of travel. When we go away, we have someone look after them, feed them, and we leave instructions in case there is a problem.

*J:* Can you think back and tell us about a few of the animals you adopted.

*Angel:* Cuddles was fourteen years old when his owner brought him to a shelter, saying he couldn't feed him any more. It turned out that the real issue was that Cuddles had cancer. So we brought him home and gave him a comfortable and caring place for the final three months of his life. Of course we shed some tears when he died, but we knew we gave him comfort and we would see him again some day.

*Joe:* Belinda was the first older cat we brought into our lives. She was over ten years old when she followed us home one day.

*Angel:* Then there was Tatiana. She was a fifteen year old cat whose owner had to go into a nursing home. The owner was terribly upset about giving up her cat, so we said we would take care of the pet. Tatiana lived another four years with us. She was 19 years old when she died.

*J:* What are some of the rewards for adopting these animals?

*Angel:* Think of being in your 80s, afraid and lost. That is how we see the older animals in the shelter. It is rewarding to see them settle in and relax in our home. We also know we give them a daily routine or structure on which they can depend.

*Joe:* It is great to discover each of their individual personalities. They are all different. Some even act like kittens at times.

*J:* What are some of the problems?

*Joe:* They won't be around forever, but nothing is permanent. You have to be prepared to deal with their passing.

*Angel:* We shed tears for all of them, but we know we gave them a loving environment that put them at ease.

*J:* Who probably should not adopt older and special needs animals and why?

*Joe:* This is not for families with young children that want a higher energy pet. It also is not for the children who will have a very difficult time with the loss of the animal.

*J:* What would you like to say to people who are considering adopting an older or special needs pet from our shelter?

*Angel:* You need to be confident that you will do what you can and not feel guilty when you can do no more. You need to keep things in perspective. You need to know that not everything the vet says can be done for the animal should necessarily be done in every case. You need to know in your heart that you made a positive difference in this animal's final life passage.

## An Everyday "Hero," Daisy Mae's Tiny Tale
(April 10, 2009)

It was one of those windy days we have been having lately, and the door blew wide open. Someone in the family rushing off to work or school hadn't shut it tightly. The little white dog peered out of the opening, sniffed all those wonderful spring smells, and stood quietly with a look of curiosity. She had never been out without her owner Patty, and Patty always held onto the other end of her leash. But this moment was exciting, and so she ventured out into the wind. Her white curly fur blew across her eyes but she trotted out the open door with confidence and headed toward a very busy street ahead.

At the same time Daisy Mae slipped out, Patty's neighbor, Warren was backing out of his driveway. From the corner of his eye, he saw the little Shih tzu. He turned around, picked her up and drove her back to her home where he shut the door tightly before going on his way. This may seem like a small thing, but in these days when neighbors are rarely even acquainted and where people feel it is best not to get involved, Warren's deed is worth mentioning. It is the small things that can really make a difference. Thanks, Warren, from Patty and Daisy Mae.

## Pit Bulls: Vicious or Beloved, but Misunderstood?
(April 17, 2009)

A member of the Friends of the Saratoga County Animal Shelter recently asked me if I would devote my column this week to the highly controversial category of dogs commonly called "Pits" or "Pit Bulls." Since a fair number of dogs labeled "pit bull terrier mixes" come through the shelter, it seems appropriate for me to discuss the myths and the realities surrounding these dogs.

Pit Bull is a catchall term for short-haired, muscular, and powerful mixed-breed dogs that may resemble recognized breeds such as the Bull Terrier, the Staffordshire Bull Terrier and/or the American Staffordshire Terrier. Pit Bulls are not a breed of dog, but rather are a category of dogs that were historically, and unfortunately in some regions, still made to fight in pits as "entertainment." Dog-fighting rings are illegal today, but tragically they still occur behind closed doors.

People who have an opinion about pit bulls either adore them or they abhor them and want them banned. Those who are fans of pit bulls describe them as sweet, loyal, smart, intuitive, and great with kids. On the other hand, those who want them banned see them as unpredictable, dangerous, untrustworthy, vicious, and frightening. How can there be such a marked difference of opinion? Part of the answer can be found by looking at their reputation over time.

American Pit Bull Terriers (APBT) were once symbols of dignity, strength, and loyalty. Their image appeared on patriotic posters in WWI and on three different covers of Life Magazine. They also stood for trustworthiness and were called "nanny dogs." Think back to Petey, the dog in Little Rascals, or Tige the dog on Buster Brown shoes. I am dating myself, but I clearly remember these dogs as American Pit Bull Terriers. They contributed to a positive image of the Pit Bull.

There also were many important people who owned American Pit Bull Terriers. Theodore Roosevelt, Thomas Edison, John Steinbeck, Humphrey Bogart, Helen Keller, and Fred Astaire were just a few who wanted to own this category of dog. So what happened to make the American Pit Bull Terrier fall from grace? What are the associations with these dogs in recent times?

Sadly, Pit Bulls have become symbols of gangs, thugs, and criminals who use them to bolster their image as tough guys. They parade their pit bulls almost as if they were loaded guns. If the dogs are walked, it is to make the owner look formidable and when they are chained up for long hours alone, it is to make people stay away from the owner's property. The dogs are encouraged to be aggressive. Pit bulls may even be beaten regularly to toughen them up, and they are rewarded for combative behavior.

How much of the Pit Bull's current reputation for aggression is in the biology of the dog and how much is due to the handler? Biologically speaking, Pit Bulls have been bred for muscular bodies including tremendously powerful jaws that can clamp down on prey and hold tight. This is a reflection of their being selected for success in the fighting arena. In other words, the potential is there for great harm if the animal is encouraged to fulfill that biological potential. And that is where the human comes into the picture. It is a bit like the old nature vs. nurture debate.

Owners of Pit Bulls need to be vigilant about being the pack leader. They need to train the dog, exercise her regularly, and pay attention to, and correct any signs of dominance over other dogs, children, or adults. The dog must know that their owner is the one in charge. For some, this will come naturally and for others, they will have to work at being the leader. These warnings can apply to handling any dog, but it is even more critical when it comes to powerful groups like Pit Bull Terriers, Rottweilers, German Shepherds, or Doberman Pinschers.

One of the best ways to socialize Pit Bulls can be seen on the National Geographic Channel's "The Dog Whisperer." Cesar Millan helps owners to be calm and assertive with their Pit Bulls and other "Gladiator" dogs. In fact, if you want to see a couple of wonderfully calm and submissive

Pit Bulls, check out his dogs, Daddy and Junior. Cesar Millan has also written several informative books on the topic.

I have no doubt that Pit Bulls can make wonderful pets. The potential owner, however, must be willing to work with the dog so that it will be socialized, not for fighting other dogs in a pit, but for a happy life as a member of a loving family.

"Out of the Pits" is an animal rescue organization specifically for Pit Bulls. The organization is dedicated to educating the public about the Pit Bull and finding homes for many displaced Pit Bulls. For more information about this organization visit www.outofthepits.org.

## Three Families and Their Adopted Shelter Pets
(April 24, 2009)

After last week's serious topic of Pit Bulls, this week I thought I would go a little lighter by introducing three local families and the pets they adopted from the Saratoga County Animal Shelter. Each of the three adopted pets will tell, in their own words, how they happily found a "forever home" and became an important member of their "forever family." First, we meet Luna, the cat with the most beautiful eyes. She tells us how Scott and Emily Martin brought her home in Sept. of 2007. Next, we hear from Baxter, a beagle that was adopted in 2008 by Deb Hall and her family. Baxter explains why he is not a typical Beagle. Finally, Sparky tells her story of landing a loving home back in 1994, and how she became a seafaring dog with sailing enthusiasts and owners Alan and Joyce Bartlett.

## 1. Luna, The Elegant Cat With Mystical Eyes

My name is Luna and I am a very classy cat that found myself in an animal shelter, no less! It must have been some grave mistake since I am of royal blood and I am exceptionally beautiful. I have been told my eyes are exquisite. So when I found myself in the shelter, I became very anxious to get out for more stylish accommodations. Once I spotted Emily and Scott walking down the rows of cages, I knew these were the ones and I made my move. I cleverly stuck my paw out through the bars and managed to tightly grab onto Scott's shirt. My next move was to meow with conviction—"don't go, don't go! I don't belong here! Take me home with you!" Scott felt compelled to open the cage and suddenly I leapt out, landing gracefully on his chest. I am a little thing, but I held on tightly because I knew I was actually a princess that deserved to find a place of comfort and style with this lovely young couple.

Style and comfort was what I found with Scott and Emily. I sit by Emily and listen to her read her poetry. I curl up by Scott and listen to him talk of legal issues and real estate opportunities. I also amuse myself by playing soccer with bottle caps, by fetching and hiding plastic ties or rubber bands, by walking on the computer keys when they are in use, and by boldly drinking water from the tap. But what I enjoy most is finding shiny pieces of jewelry, carrying them to my food bowl, and one by one I drop them into the bowl. I often end up with a considerable collection of lovely jewels by the end of the day. Yes, life is good for me now. Scott and Emily treat me the way a refined lady of royalty should be treated. And I give back lots of affection and a few good-natured mischievous moments, like when I knocked over wastebaskets and artistically scattered the contents throughout the house.

## 2. Baxter, The Not-So-Typical Beagle

I have been told it is common knowledge that Beagles, left to their own devices, will become overweight because they love to eat so much, and they have a bark or howl that is ear-piercing. Well, if being a chowhound and making lots of noise is typical of my breed, I am a not-so-typical Beagle. I am not particularly food-driven and I am not inclined to bark or howl. But I am getting ahead of myself. Let me tell my story of finding a forever home in the summer of 2008 with Deb and Darren Hall, and the four kids---17 years old, Kristcha, 15 years old, Danielle, 11 years old, Nick, and 8 years old, Erika. I love them all and they love me, except maybe Kristcha who has a love/hate relationship with me because when I want attention, I systematically take her things off her dresser. But that is my only bad habit, according to Deb.

Before Deb adopted me, I was found running loose and frightened on Rt. 29. Some very nice animal control officers saved me from getting hurt in all the traffic and took me to the county animal shelter. When it became clear that no one was coming to claim me, I was put up for adoption. Lots of people looked me over and called me a "Snoopy dog." I never figured out what a Snoopy dog was, but two different families put their names on a list of interested people. Then Deb came along and added her name. She did not think she had a chance since there were two names ahead of her, but she still had hope. I guess I really impressed her by sitting on command and by being calm, even in that hectic shelter environment. Later she said she wanted a calm dog because her large family shared a somewhat chaotic lifestyle.

On the fourth of July, the shelter people called Deb and said I was hers if she was still interested. They also told her that I tested positive for Lyme disease. Deb was not deterred by the Lyme disease and brought me home. Well, the first three days I got very sick and I worried that Deb would take me back to the shelter. But instead of returning me, she took me to the Vet who gave me shots and pills. In 24 hours I was all better and back to my playful self. Since then things have been good with the Halls. I do not chew things, I do not steal food, I never mess inside, I can be trusted alone in the house, I play nicely in the back yard with Nick's old football, and I am a people person. The only time I growl is in my sleep when I dream. I don't mean to sound like a bragger, but I am a pretty wonderful pet. I look forward to many years with the Halls where I can stay close to them. A few members of the family even let me curl up to sleep with my head resting on their shoulders and neck.

### 3. Sparky, The Ship's Dog

Sixteen years ago I was born into a large litter of Springer Spaniel and Labrador mix puppies. When we were about six months old we were taken to the county animal shelter where we all tried to impress the people coming through in search of the perfect puppy. When Alan and Joyce Bartlett came up and watched us for over an hour, they picked me because I was not too dominant nor was I too submissive. Alan said I was just right. Little did I know then that life with Alan and Joyce would include the thrill of sailing and the opportunity for me to be a ship's dog! Of course when I was very young, I had to learn about the sea and boats before I was worthy of the title.

The first time Alan and Joyce took me to Mystic, I stepped off the dock thinking it was going to be shallow water below, but to my shock it was deep and I was never a great swimmer. So they stood there laughing as I splashed about trying to regain my composure. But I learned from that startling experience, and later when I accidentally pushed a perfectly delicious bone off the dock, I knew I could only watch helplessly as it disappeared into the deep dark seawater. Then, when Alan and Joyce took me on their

34-foot sailboat for the first time, I was "sick as a dog." But that was the one and only time I got seasick, because after that, I got my sea legs.

Soon I became an old hand at life on the ocean. I sat on the upper deck of our sailboat, smelled the salty sea air, and felt the breeze on my face. When we needed supplies from the shore towns, Alan and Joyce took me with them in the dingy, and I always stood proudly at the bow. In fact, after awhile I even became a tourist attraction. In Plymouth Harbor, Massachusetts, there was a tour boat that came around every hour. The tour director would point me out standing on the bow while the tourists would clap and take pictures.

I went everywhere with Alan and Joyce. When the ship was in dry storage and they worked on maintenance and repairs, I would climb up the ladder behind Alan and he would carry me back down. When he was in a hurry and needed to make several trips up and down, he decided to leave me up there until he could climb back up again. I would not stand for that and just jumped all the way down on my own. The landing was hard but I never wanted to let Alan out of my sight. After all, he was my captain, and I was the ship's dog.

## Children and Dog Bites
(May 1, 2009)

I have a wonderful Black Lab service dog named Vida. She has been with me for over nine years. We go everywhere together. She comes with me to the nursing home when I visit my 94-year-old mother, she comes with me to the grocery store, and she comes with me to the YMCA when I swim in the mornings. Since I am in a wheelchair full time, she helps me when something is out of reach by picking up the item in her teeth and dropping it onto my lap. She is a wonderful canine companion and one of the gentlest souls I have ever known.

Because of her nature and her training, I never worry when children come up to pet Vida. I tell them and their parents that it is best always to ask first, but sometimes little ones just cannot resist running up to Vida and enthusiastically throwing their arms around her neck or her chest. But not all dogs are calm like Vida, and so I worry that in another situation the outcome could be very different. Last Saturday at the Geyser Rd. Elementary School's health fair, Vida and I sat at the booth for the Friends of the Saratoga County Animal Shelter and I saw lots of children who wanted to meet Vida. Along with other information and giveaways we handed out information sheets about approaching dogs safely.

There are over one million dog bites annually in the United States. The majority of these bites involve children. Surprisingly, children are more likely to be bitten by their family dog or by the neighbor's dog than by a strange dog. There are some common sense rules that parents need to teach their children about approaching any dog, even familiar dogs owned by the child's family, and even with gentle Vida.

Children should always ask their parents and the owner of the dog before approaching the animal.

The owner should have the dog sit politely before the child reaches to pet it. If the owner cannot control the dog in this way, the parent and child should abort the plan and move along.

- Kids need to be taught to let a dog sniff them first before reaching out to pet the dog.
- Children need to know never to wake a sleeping dog because a startled dog is more likely to bite.

- A dog with puppies should never be approached without adult supervision.
- A dog behind a fence, a dog in a car, or a dog on a chain should never be approached.
- Kids need to understand that teasing a dog with a stick or any other object is asking for trouble.
- Children should be taught never to try petting a dog when it is eating because this can trigger food aggression.
- Parents who walk with their child in a stroller need to be aware that their child's face is often right at a dog's level and in close range. It is best to steer clear of passing dogs in this case.
- If a dog chases a child, that child needs to know to stop, stand still, resist screaming and avoid looking directly into the dog's eyes. Then they need to slowly walk away facing the dog, but again not focusing on the eyes.
- If a child is attacked, they should drop, curl up like a ball and cover their head and face with their arms and hands.

Having these important conversations with children is a little tricky because you do not want the child to be terrified of dogs, but rather the hope is that they learn to respect dogs and they become a bit more cautious and smart about them.

## It's All About The Animals
(May 8, 2009)

The good people who work at the Saratoga County Animal Shelter have a tremendously challenging job. For example, they need to keep their cool when an angry dog owner comes in to pick up his dog after it was rescued from running loose in traffic. Rather than expressing gratitude for the safe return of the animal, these owners respond with anger over the inconvenience to them and the fine they must pay.

Handling pets that have been abused or neglected is another stressful aspect of the job. Since most shelter workers are attracted to the job because they have a fondness for animals, seeing the results of abuse or neglect can be terribly disturbing. I can only imagine that a shelter worker has to develop a thick skin and an ability to leave the stress and emotion at work rather than bringing it home at the end of the day.

Cleaning out the kennels, day in and day out, is something that must be done every morning before 10 am when the shelter opens, and every afternoon after 4 pm when it closes. The employees must also work the desk and answer calls, often responding to the same questions again and again. They also may need to bathe dogs that come in from the streets. In a small shelter like our county shelter, every employee must learn all of the tasks. Cross-training is essential. So how do they do it all and manage to keep from becoming discouraged or even burned out? I posed this question to Dan Butler, the shelter Supervisor, because Dan knows first-hand about burnout in shelter work. A look at his long career, his seven-year break from it, and his vision today for the future of the county shelter is a story of patience, hard work, commitment, and renewal.

Dan was destined to work with animals. Beginning as a 5th grader, he regularly helped out the local veterinarian, Dr. Elmer Robinson. Further, when his dad was the chief financial officer for Skidmore College, Dan lived with his seven siblings and his parents in the Scribner House on North Broadway. There they had a menagerie of animals including rabbits, cats, dogs, fish, and birds. They even had crowing roosters and a hen that lived in the carriage house, on North Broadway, no less! In short, animals and their care made up a large part of Dan's youth.

When the Saratoga County Animal Shelter was first built in 1978, Dan was one of three shelter workers. He recalls that back then, there were more puppies and kittens because people were less likely to spay or neuter their animals. He also remembers that it was rare for older animals to be adopted. At the same time, there were fewer animal rescue organizations, and there were fewer individual volunteers that could help with the animals. For twenty years, Dan worked under these difficult conditions. Then in 1999, he knew he needed to leave the shelter for his well being and the well being of the people around him. After seven years away from the shelter, working "with great groups of guys" in the public works department, Dan was reinvigorated and ready to come back to the shelter world.

Dan feels that over the years there have been signs of positive change in public opinions concerning animals and adoption. He also finds that there are more people wanting to volunteer at the shelter, there are many more rescue groups forming in the area, and there is interest in supporting a new building to replace the old shelter that had become outdated and inadequate. Things are looking up for the shelter and the animals. Dan fueled his revitalized energy to help design a new shelter, to work creatively with volunteers, and to engage with the many rescue organizations.

Today, Dan has a staff of five full-time and four part-time employees. He also has a team of volunteer dog walkers that take the dogs out for walks so the animals can get a break from their pens. Other volunteers take cats to malls, senior citizen centers, and other locations for off-site adoption clinics. Dan also gets help placing animals with the several rescue groups. In addition, there are donors who have helped with the costs of spaying and neutering, other needed medical procedures, and raised beds for the animals. Friends of the Saratoga County Animal Shelter, the fundraising arm of the shelter, have been instrumental in many of these initiatives that call for sustained fundraising.

After interviewing Dan, I began to realize that, in him, the shelter workers and the volunteers have a wonderful role model. Dan was smart enough to know when he needed a break from the shelter. He also knew when he was renewed and able to come back with a more positive vision and a deeper understanding of the day-to-day challenges that can take a toll. We are all very glad you are back, Dan! Furthermore, I am sure the staff and volunteers appreciate his understanding that each of them will find their own way to thrive and survive the challenges of shelter work. They can also remind themselves of Dan's words, "Above everything else, it is all about the animals; it's always about the animals."

## Max, Vida, and Sully
(May 15, 2009)

A couple of times in Whiskers and Tales, I have referred to my beloved service dog, Vida. Vida is now over eleven years old, she is fit and trim, but she is slowing down and now she has quite a bit of grey around her muzzle. The average life expectancy for a Lab is 11-12 years, but some live to be 13 or even 14 years. Of course I hope for her longevity, but at the same time, I am thinking she deserves an honorable retirement. With that in mind, I began the process of looking for another dog that Vida and I can train to do the things she does for me.

I let my friends at the Saratoga County Animal Shelter know what I was looking for in another dog. Soon I learned of a dog named Max. My husband Steve, Vida, and I went to the shelter to see this Rottweiler mix. His head looks pure Rottie but the rest of him could be German Shepherd and/or Akita. His tail looks Shepherd when it hangs down, but at attention it curls up on his back like an Akita. It might sound like a strange combination and a show dog enthusiast would probably just shake his head and sigh, but actually the combination works aesthetically, making Max a very handsome dog indeed.

After Vida and Max greeted each other, the way dogs do—noses to butts, Vida choose to ignore him and seemed aloof about the whole matter. Then we needed to see how Max would react to my wheelchair. Some dogs are funny about medical equipment, but Max was not bothered at all. He even eagerly walked alongside my chair and me. Twice he got too close and my wheel pinched his toes, but he didn't make a sound and just moved forward with a bit more care. At first he was described to us as neutered, so when a shelter worker said he was not altered yet, I said he must be mistaken. The shelter worker reached under Max and said with a grin, "my hands do not lie; this boy has not been neutered."

My initial impression of Max was that he is smart, eager to please, affectionate, and with considerable training, he has the makings of a wonderful canine companion and service dog. The only thing that we still needed to check on was that he and our 2-year-old rescued shelter cat, Sully (nicknamed Twitch), would get along. At first I kept Max on a leash until it seemed safe to let him off. It turned out that after 48 hours of stand-offs, hissing, and chasing around the house, the two of them settled down and now the cat tolerates Max, while all he wants to do is play, but he is learning it must be cautious, respectful play.

Of course this is just the beginning of our relationship with Max and each week I will provide an update on how things are progressing with training, the neutering, and with the hints Max gives us about his unknown past. I will also report on Vida and Sully as they deal with the job of helping me teach Max more about manners and service. Whenever we bring a new animal into our families, it is a journey of discovery and adjustment for everyone involved. I look forward to sharing the ups and downs of that journey with the readers of Whiskers and Tales.

## Beau and Bella, Two Maine Coon Cats
(May 29, 2009)

Originally a working cat (superior mouser), the Maine Coon cat is solid, rugged, and can tolerate harsh New England winters. Distinctive characteristics include tufted ears, a smooth shaggy waterproof coat, large round snowshoe feet and a long fluffy tail. They are some of the largest domestic North American cats ranging between 14-18 lbs. for males and 9-12 lbs. for females. Maine Coon cat owners often describe them as affectionate, funny, and very smart. My friends Richard Wilkinson and Susan Bender would agree that "Mainies" have delightful personalities. For the past 7 years, Dick and Sue shared their home with two Maine Coon cats, Beau and Bella.

Beau and Bella were affectionate, funny, and smart, but they also taught Dick and Sue a profound lesson about the interconnectedness of life, death, and compassion. These lessons followed the passing of Beau. Dick wrote about it in a poignant essay and kindly agreed to let me quote part of it here:

> On the day before we were to leave for London, Beau's heart condition turned suddenly worse. Calls to the vet resulted in the suggestion we take him to an emergency clinic for either drastic measures or putting down. We instead decided to wait and see

what course nature had in mind for him. Eventually he struggled to his feet, and made his wobbly way to the basement, a favorite haunt. He was followed by his sister, Bella. A bit later I went down to see how he was doing, and couldn't find him [we have one of those basements]. I finally found Bella sitting still and staring at something or someone under the stairs. Of course it was Beau, who had found a place of his own, and died. I wrapped Beau in a sheet and left him there, as it was late and there was nothing else to be done. Bella remained with him for some time. I then packed up his bed and put it away. Bella found the bed, and somehow indicated it should be put in a more open space. I followed her directive, and she ended up lying next to it for the night.

There have been similar "spooky" incidences since, and it is abundantly clear to me that Bella is grieving her lost brother. I was not ready to accept this kind of "human" behavior from a cat—not even our obviously brilliant cat. Graduate school had taught me to be a trained skeptic, and the training took, but I now have a painfully obvious example of the continuum. I do not feel, "How wonderful; the cat is really human-like," as many people say when they learn of a chimpanzee's linguistic, tool-making, hunting and social skills. What I feel is how much we all share in this life, how much a part of a grander thing we all are; Darwin might have agreed with his famous statement, "there is a grandeur in this view of life." I find myself considering Bella with a new vision: I thank Beau for this powerful enlightenment, and I wonder: what next? Richard Wilkinson

What came next was after a respectable period of mourning; Dick and Sue adopted a kitten from the Saratoga County Animal Shelter. The kitten was just 6 weeks old when they brought him home to Bella. They named him Bertie and describe him as spunky. Bella was not impressed with the little guy and in fact, she wanted nothing to do with him. Nevertheless, he was undaunted by her lack of interest and continues to try to win her over. After three weeks, Bella is tolerating the kitten. Perhaps over time she will even come to enjoy Bertie, but at this point, the best we can say is that at least Bella is no longer depressed about her brother Beau.

---

## Follow-Up On Three Pet Stories
(May 29, 2009)

Hey, its Jill's dog, Vida. You know, the one in the photo with her. Yep, that's me, the handsome black lab. She's not feeling too great today, so I am finishing up this week's Whiskers and Tales for her. We have several stories that need follow-ups, so here they are:

Let's start with Sparky, the ship's dog. On May 18, Sparky passed over to the other side. People get really sad when this happens, but I know she is now having fun in the Great Dog Park where all dogs run and play without the pain of old age, where there are no dog fights, and where we will all meet up again someday. Owners Alan and Joyce Bartlett wrote this about Sparky ...

It is with great sadness we report the passing of Sparky, a sixteen-year-old Springer Spaniel mix adopted from Saratoga County Animal Shelter in 1994. Sparky was a featured rescued dog in the April 24, 2009 issue of Pet Corner (see Sparky, the ship's dog). She resided all of her life with the Bartlett's in Malta, NY, recently spending her winters in Mount Holly, VT with the Gower family. Sparky sailed widely from Cape Cod to Long Island. She was a loyal companion who was loved by all who knew her and will be greatly missed.

Sparky was a good girl and we miss her already.

Moving right along, there is a follow-up on Bella, the Maine Coon cat that lost her brother, Beau. Bella still hasn't shown any affection for Bertie, the new kitten, but at least now she will tolerate being in the same room with him. Bertie is still happy-go-lucky and pays no heed to Bella's lack of friendliness. Owners Sue and Dick found out about a book (Cat Vs. Cat by Pam Johnson-Bennett) that deals with the issue of introducing a new cat into the family. So maybe that will give them some ideas to try. What is really interesting, however, is that Dick buried Beau under the bird feeder where he always liked to sit (but never caught any birds.) Bella never sat there before, but now that Beau is buried there she spends hours sleeping on his grave under the bird feeder. Yep, Bella keeps challenging Dick and Sue (both are anthropologists) about animal behavior and grieving.

Last but not least there is a follow-up on Max, Sully and me. This I will ask Jill to write because I am biased and might have a hard time reporting fairly on the situation.

### Update on Max, Vida, and Sully

Things do not always work out as we plan. I thought I would be writing an update this week about how nicely everything was falling into place with our three pets, but the story took a drastic turn after Max had been with us for three weeks.

Three weeks was all it took for Max to really settle in and feel at home. The training was going great and I loved how affectionate he was with both my husband and me. Vida and the cat avoided him most of the time and everything was peaceful. But what started to be a problem was Max's growing need to be first in all things. He had to go out the door first, he had to get into the car first, he had to drink from the water bowls first, he had to get a cookie first, and he had to get my attention first. But this was not insurmountable because I was already teaching him the command, WAIT and training him to wait until I went out, or until Vida went out, etc. Nevertheless, needing to be first was symbolic of a larger dominance issue. The more at home and relaxed Max got, the more we saw his need to dominate.

Once again, I felt this was manageable until Max suddenly attacked Vida as they both stood by the sink, waiting for me to fill the water bowls. There was no blood, only tooth marks on Vida's check and ear, but soon they became infected and she needed antibiotics before the swelling went down. When it happened there was lots of noise from both of them—Max with growls and barks and Vida with cries and whimpers. As soon as it happened, I grabbed Max by the scruff of the neck and pulled him off her. He backed away with a surprised look on his face, but he kept his distance while I checked her over.

The worst part of this incident was that Vida, who doesn't have a dominant bone in her body became so afraid of Max that from that point on she refused to go out into the yard if he was already there or come into the house if he was already inside. She wouldn't pass him in the hall to get to her bed or enter my room, where she always slept. In fact, she just seemed to shut down.

What should we do about the matter? At first I thought we should wait a week until Max's vet appointment to be neutered. Being neutered might help the situation, but there are no guarantees and what if, while we wait for the surgery, there was another, more serious incident? Steve and I agonized over the situation, but Vida's' reaction convinced us that keeping Max was not fair to her. After all, she spent nine years as my service dog, and she is now a senior citizen that deserves a peaceful retirement.

The whole experience was a heartbreaker, but it also was a learning situation. I learned from my dog trainer friend that if there will be a problem with an adoption, it typically happens around the third week when pets and people let down their guard. I also learned it is important to trust my instincts, especially when it comes to the animals. Only now I can admit to myself that I saw some signs of trouble earlier on, but I ignored them because I wanted so much for Max to fit into our family.

I know Max will find his forever home, but I think he needs to be an "only child." He is smart, affectionate, eager to please, and very handsome. I took him back to the shelter after some tears and reassurances from my friends there who said that Steve and I made the right decision for Vida, for us, and even for Max who deserves to be in a home where he is top dog and the only dog.

Postscript: Good news—I just learned that Max was adopted a couple of days ago!

Well, that's it for this week. I am a happy dog now that the bully is gone, and I have no desire to retire from my service job looking after Jill. I may have grey whiskers, but there are still plenty of good times in me before I go to the Great Dog Park! Cheers, Vida

---

## Summertime, When The Liv'in Is Easy
(June 5, 2009)

Yes, summer is finally here after another long northeast winter. Now it is time to enjoy the outdoors without all the coats, scarves, gloves and hats we must pile on every time we go out in the bitter cold. My favorite things about summer include (1) being out-of-doors in the sunshine and warmth, (2) swimming and boating in lakes or in the ocean, (3) gardening, (4) farmers' market, and (5) Fourth of July celebrations. Each of these five summertime activities can be great fun, but they can also mean trouble for your pets. So if you see summer as a time to take your pets out for new adventures (and I hope you do), be prepared to protect them from a multitude of situations they might encounter.

### 1. Being out-of-doors in sunshine and warmth

Both cats and dogs can get too much sun and heat. Neither of them perspires to cool down their bodies. Rather, they must pant to regulate their body temperature, but as the temperature rises, the panting cannot evacuate heat quickly enough, and the body temperature will continue to rise to dangerous levels. Heat exhaustion and heat stroke can result and in extreme cases can cause damage to the pet's kidneys, liver, intestinal tract, heart, and brain. This can be a life-threatening situation.

The leading cause of heat exhaustion and heat stroke is leaving a pet in the car on a summer day. Even on a mild day when the temperature is 75 degrees, the temperature in the car can quickly rise to 130 degrees. Leaving the windows slightly open will not prevent the heat build-up. Other factors that contribute to the problem are humidity, lack of ventilation, and pet anxiety. Also dark-colored pets, older pets and very young pets will suffer sooner because their ability to regulate body temperature is hindered. Even some breeds of dogs and cats (like the bulldog or the Persian cat) that have been bred to have a "cute" pushed-in face, are more likely to suffer from the heat because their airways are compromised.

Heat stroke also can occur when a pet is outside with no shade and no water. Further, strenuous exercise on a hot day can result in heat stroke. Some dogs will play "until they drop." If you have a dog like this, you need to step in and stop the play periodically and encourage the animal to rest in the shade and drink some water. Owners need to be sure there is shade and plenty of fresh clear water at all times. Hot days also encourage people to let their dog keep his head out the window of a moving car or let him stand in the back of a moving pick-up truck. The result can be flying debris becoming lodged in the eyes or ears, and dogs in the back of a pick-up can be thrown off balance and land in a busy street.

Signs of pet heat stroke include discolored gums, flushed red ears, elevated heart rate, furious panting, vomiting, disorientation, diarrhea, and a wobbly gait. If you suspect your pet is suffering from the heat, act immediately to lower the body temperature by wetting the animal with a hose, submersing it in cool (not cold) water, or place wet towels over the body. Next call the veterinarian.

One owner of a longhaired dog decided it would be best for the dog to have his hair shaved off for the summer. The result was serious sunburn. Cats can also get sunburns on the tips of their ears and their mouths. Spending time outdoors can also mean pets may cross paths with other animals. If you have ever had your dog or cat investigate a porcupine or a skunk, you know what terrible trouble can ensue. For all these reasons, fun in the sun for your pets should be supervised.

One final point: during summer, kids and workmen go in and out of the house frequently, leaving doors ajar or gates unlatched. The result can be an escape for a pet. Be sure your pet has identification such as a tag, a collar with a stitched phone number, a microchip, or an identifying tattoo. In addition, be sure to call the local animal shelter and/or the animal control officers to find your pet.

### 2. Swimming and boating in lakes and in the ocean

Not all dogs are good swimmers. Some breeds have slightly webbed feet and are great swimmers, but others must struggle to stay afloat. To be safe, some boat owners will place their dog in a lifejacket when riding in their boat. Along lake or ocean shores dogs can gulp too much salt water, pick up sand fleas, get into rotting fish, play with a washed-up jellyfish, or roll in other good smelling garbage.

Many years ago, I took my Fox terrier mix to June Lake in the California High Sierras. He sat in the canoe while I fished. We were having a delightful time until I realized my dog was fixated on the cheese I was putting on my fishhook. To my horror, I looked down to see he had swallowed both the cheese bait and hook. We drove two hours to the closest vet who took x-rays and concluded that the hook made its way to the stomach where it would dissolve naturally. Phew, that was a close call!

When it comes to swimming in a pool, pets should never be free to swim without supervision. Filters and pool grates can be dangerous to a dog (or a child) as well as the chemicals commonly used to keep the water clean. All chemicals need to be carefully stored and after a swim in a pool, dogs should be rinsed off, especially if they are prone to rashes or other skin conditions.

### 3. Gardening

When I think about gardening, I think about mulch, flowers, fertilizer, and all the insects that can be pests to pets (and humans). Heartworm, Lyme disease, ticks and fleas can all make our animals uncomfortable and even very sick. Every spring pet owners need to bring their animals to the vet for an annual checkup and for advice on the prevention of illnesses carried by insects. Even indoor cats can be exposed to diseases carried by insects.

Gardening and lawn care also bring to mind fertilizers and chemicals that may be poison to your pets. Pay attention to the little flags marking recent chemical treatments that could be harmful to your pet's paws. In addition, educate yourself about the plants in your yard to be sure they are not poisonous if ingested. Keep handy the phone number for the Animal Poison Control Center: (888) 426 4435.

### 4. Farmers' Market

There is nothing better than a trip to the local farmers' market in the summer. Everywhere I look, I see beautiful produce, old friends, colorful flowers, and hard-working farmers. The crowds of people all seem happy to be out under the tents making their purchases. People bring their children and their dogs, including many that seem like they have never been in such a chaotic and busy place. So what is the problem here? The problem is simply that many of the dogs have no manners, and their owners are too busy making purchases to notice that periodically two or more dogs will get into a confrontation. I am concerned about the children who could find themselves in the middle of a dog challenge. People need to have control over their dogs in the crowded farmers' market so no one suffers from a dog bite.

### 5. Fourth of July celebrations

Many pets become very nervous when they hear fireworks. These are the same dogs that find electrical storms terrifying. If you must leave a dog like this home alone during fireworks or electrical storms, leave the television or radio on and ask a neighbor to check on them. Too often a panicked pet will turn their fear into a destructive rampage. If the dog has been crate-trained and is used to being left in a crate, this is probably the best way to protect your furnishings.

My goal here is not to make everyone sick with worry, but rather to disseminate information that could save your pet's life. Much of it is common sense, but it does not hurt to remind ourselves periodically so we can be responsible pet owners and safely enjoy the wonders of summer with our pets.

## Presidents and First Dogs
(June 12, 2009)

When a president of a small college or a president of an entire nation owns a dog, he seems a little more approachable, a little more down-to-earth, and a little more like the rest of us. Ironically, it is the dog that makes the man (or woman) more human. Perhaps this is why there is so much public interest in the dog that becomes a "first dog." Only a few weeks ago, there was media frenzy when President Barack Obama and first lady Michelle Obama finally decided on the dog they would bring into the White House. I had never heard of a Portuguese Waterdog before, but now at least I know what one looks like. After viewing the television showing the first family and Bo, the new puppy, I thought President Obama looked a bit uncomfortable interacting with the animal. Perhaps President Obama did not grow up with dogs and is not comfortable with them. Nevertheless, he delivered on his promise of a dog for his girls anyway. Could it also be that these days U.S. Presidents are expected to get a dog?

Closer to home, at Skidmore College there is another president and first lady with a first dog all living in the Scribner House on North Broadway.

President Phillip Glotzbach and his wife, Marie have a chocolate Labrador Retriever named Summit. President Glotzbach is the first Skidmore College president to have a dog while in office. Phil had dogs all his life and in 1988,

Marie surprised the family at Christmas with a shelter puppy. That puppy grew up and lived with them until his passing in 2001. By the time they accepted their Skidmore positions, however, the Glotzbachs were without a canine companion.

Phil and Marie knew that a new puppy would be too hard on the lovely old Scribner House, so in 2004 when their son told them about a trained three-year-old Lab that needed a home, they were more then interested. Soon arrangements were made and Summit traveled from New Orleans to his new home with Phil and Marie. He quickly adapted to his new owners and his new environment. Summit found his forever home and soon Skidmore students and staff fell in love with him.

Summit has a great life. He gets a walk, a run, or a tennis ball retrieving session twice a day. Occasionally he even gets to ride in the car up to the Adirondacks for a swim in a lake and a hike on a trail. Sometimes he even gets to go to the office with Phil or meet a group of students at the Scribner House. When the Glotzbachs have to travel on Skidmore business, Summit has several wonderful dog sitters who take him to their homes while Phil and Marie are away. One of these dog sitters is Jennifer Finnegan

According to Jennifer, "Summit is a happy-go-lucky dog that loves people and tennis balls." Jen went on to describe him as a handsome boy that will fetch the tennis ball until the thrower can throw no more. When Summit is staying with Jennifer, she brings him to work at the Skidmore Colton House where he begins his morning by going around to see everyone who works there and then quietly lies down under Jennifer's desk, as close as he can get to her feet.

I had the opportunity to talk with President Glotzbach about Summit. Much of what he said confirmed for me that if we are tuned into our pets, we can learn from them.

Phil explained that Summit is grounded, centered, and calming. He said Summit has a zen-like quality about him that is contagious. Phil also said that Summit reminds him of the need for discipline in life. Zen-like calmness, discipline and contentment seem to be a part of Summit's character and appeal.

Okay, so what is wrong with Summit? He cannot be all that perfect, can he? Well, there are two issues that keep him from being perfect. First, Phil says he is a little vain about how he looks—"he is handsome and he knows it." And the second thing is that when Summit meets another dog he gets fearful and a little aggressive. Phil believes that this is because he was never properly socialized to other dogs when he was young. Getting a dog into an obedience class with other young dogs is so important. Despite these two "flaws," Summit is a terrific dog. He is smart about knowing what humans are asking of him. He loves to fetch a tennis ball, a stick, or anything else he can get someone to throw for him. Furthermore, Summit always wants to be right up next to the people he loves, the closer, the better. And if those people are paying attention, they can learn from Summit how to be centered, calm, and disciplined.

## Parakeets or Budgies— Little Social Birds
(June 26, 2009)

Most of my articles have been about furry four-legged canine or feline pets. Today, I am switching gears to write about birds as pets, most particularly parakeets. For families that cannot have a cat or dog because of space, a landlord, or because of allergies, birds might be something to consider. Birds can be playful, amusing, and very social. Like any pet, however, there are things you should know before you bring a feathered friend home from the pet store. As a kid I enjoyed several parakeets and when I started college, I purchased sixteen breeding pairs, set up nesting boxes in a large aviary and began a breeding program. Soon I was selling the babies to local pet stores. I learned a lot from the experience and I earned enough money to pay for my textbooks.

The term "parakeet" is actually a catchall term referring to several kinds of small birds related to the parrot. The bird that most Americans refer to, as a parakeet, is actually a "budgie" or "budgerigar." Both names refer to small birds that live in the Australian bush. The British and the Australians typically use the term budgie while Americans use the term parakeet. Budgie or parakeet—these are delightful little birds that can live 8 to 10 years if they are given proper care. Proper care includes a clean cage, quality food, clean water, daily exercise, and companionship.

A parakeet can be sexed by the color of the area above the beak, surrounding the nostrils. This area is called the "cere." With adult parakeets, the cere is blue if it is a male and a brownish pink tone if it is a female. Young parakeets are harder to sex because in both young males and young females this area is a shade of purple. Experts say they still can tell because the young male's cere is slightly brighter.

The cage for a parakeet must be large enough for the bird to stretch his wings and fly a short distance. It should have bars that are narrow enough so the bird cannot get its head caught between them. The cage should have both vertical and horizontal bars for climbing. A bottom tray that pulls out will make clean-up easier and a plastic skirt helps to keep seeds from flying out and landing on the floor. The cage must be cleaned regularly and should be equipped with cuttlebone, water, seed, small pieces of fresh fruit and vegetables, and interesting objects for climbing and playing.

Parakeets need to be let out of their cage regularly. Before taking him out, be sure there are no open windows or doors. If you bought a young parakeet, you will have better luck at finger training him so he will land on your finger to be brought out of the cage, and later to be put back. It is always best to supervise these periods outside of the cage. Parakeets should be let out of their cage every day for at least an hour. Without this regular exercise parakeets can become overweight. This is particularly true if they are given seed treats soaked in honey. If you want to give your parakeet these treats, keep it a special occasion, rather than something always available to them.

What I like most about parakeets is they each have a distinctive personality, they are "monogamous," mating for life, and if there is only one of them, they will seek and find companionship with humans. Parakeets need to belong to a flock and they will see the human family as their flock if necessary. I also love the wide range of colors to be found on parakeets. When I was breeding them I had green, blue, yellow, albino, and combinations of those colors. I never had much luck training a parakeet to talk, but it can be done with patience and repetition. If you want your bird to talk, be sure not to have a mirror or another bird in the cage. With a mirror or a companion bird, they are less likely to focus on you and the words you are trying to get them to say.

Like any pet, parakeets need attention from their owners. They will not do well if they are simply left alone in their cage. They need social interaction and a variety of interesting or challenging activities. They need to explore their environment and spread their wings. If you can provide these things for them you will be rewarded with a little colorful feathered friend that can always bring you good cheer.

## Hap's Story
(July 3, 2009)

When animals are found as strays, many people devote their time and energy to find the owners. Animal control officers who work for the towns bring the animals to the shelter and the employees of the shelter, in cooperation with volunteers, veterinarians, rescue groups like H.O.P.E. and Friends of the Saratoga County Animal Shelter take part in providing for the care and well being of the animals, hopefully until they have happy reunions with the owners or until they find new forever homes. The following is a story of a stray named Hap, told in his own way...

Hi, my name is Happy (Hap for short), but I am not feeling too happy right now. I am not sure what has happened, but I have been left alone. My humans left me behind and I have nowhere to go. It is very scary being on my own and I am struggling to survive. Finding food and a place to stay dry is very hard when you are a dog. People yell at you and chase you away because they are frightened of a dog they do not know. Staying out of the rain, scrapping for food out of the trash, avoiding other animals and trying not to get hit by those big things with wheels are all quite a challenge for me. I am cold, muddy, and my fur is all matted. I also am starting to itch because I think I picked up some fleas from that old blanket I found in the garbage. I am hiding in the alley and it is very cold. Wait, there is a human coming toward me and she is talking to me. She has treats and boy, do they taste good. My new human friend's name is Channon and she is helping me into her truck. It seems we are going for a ride; I wonder where we are going.

I later learn this human who picked me up is Channon Emigh. She is the animal control officer for the town of Greenfield. I am lucky because this human also works at the Saratoga County Animal Shelter where she is taking me right now. When we arrive at the shelter Channon brings me into a room with cages. It is warm, dry, and there are some canine friends and one grumpy cat that hissed at me. After some conversing with my new friends, I found out that a dog named Jack was also brought in by Channon from Greenfield. Apparently, Channon gets calls from residents of Greenfield when they find stray dogs. Channon picks them up and if she cannot find the owners, she brings them to the shelter where he or she will be kept safe until the shelter people can find the owners. After six days, if an owner does not come for the animal, it goes up for adoption.

Another human comes in to talk to Channon. This other human is Deb Kelly who talks to me and a dog named Renee in the next cage. Deb says Renee was running away from a male dog that chased her because she is not spayed. Renee ran so far that she got lost and could not find her way back to her home. I overheard Deb and Channon say that when dogs are not spayed or neutered, they tend to wander. The grumpy old cat named Moonstar was brought in because she is limping and someone found her on the side of the road. The other male dog, Jack, is hovering in the back of his cage growling at everyone. He tells me he is scared and does not want to be in the shelter. I tell him he is safe and these people seem kind and only wanted to help us.

After spending some time in the shelter, I noticed how old and shabby it looked. I overheard the humans talk about how excited they are, and how much better things will be, once the new shelter is built later this year. That's nice, I thought, but it doesn't help us now. At least this old outdated building has people who keep it very clean. The humans take me to the office where they fill out some forms and a little office cat greets me with his fur all puffed up. I assure him I am not going to eat him. My new canine friends, Jack and Renee, as well as Moonstar the old cat, are now safe in the shelter with people who are going to take care of us.

Moonstar the cat was taken aside by a shelter employee named Melanie Bedford. Melanie brushed out Moonstar's long hair. She loved doing this because she really loves cats. Melanie then called Alicia Rendo and Ann Boisvert, two more shelter employees, to look at Moonstar's injured paw. After examining the paw, they wrote a note for the veterinarian, gave her some medicine, and helped Melanie give her some shots. Melanie also checked Moonstar for a microchip and was getting her ready to be moved into a holding area where she will stay for three days to give the vaccines a chance to work. Moving Moonstar happened just in time because Jack, Renee, and I are not too fond of cats.

Meanwhile Tracy Dussault and Cathy Ondreko worked on more forms for Renee and me. They also checked us for collars, identification and scanned us for a microchip. Next we were given a shot in the neck and they put some stuff up our noses. Yuck, that was awful. On top of all that, Tracy and Cathy treated us for fleas. I'll be glad when that kicks in so I can get rid of these pests that make me itch. Finally another staff member, Ryan Dreher who oversees the kennels signed Jack in and moved him to a quiet area because he was so scared he needed a place to chill out. Then Ryan, Tracy, and Cathy gave us a bath. Boy, did it feel good. Once we were looking better, they took our pictures to put them on the Internet in hopes that our humans might look for us online. I tried to look my best, but I was never a very handsome dog. My mother was a beagle and they say my father was a German shepherd and the result was pretty odd.

It was time to be placed in our kennels where we will wait for six days. This gives our owners an opportunity to find us. On the second day, Renees' humans came for her. There were tears of joy as her humans hugged her. Before they left, Renee had shiny new tags on her collar showing she had rabies shots. The staff also pointed out to her owners that Renee would not run as much if she was spayed.

They offered some options for low cost spay and neutering. Jack also had a happy reunion with his humans on the third day of his stay. He was a totally different dog when he saw them. He was so happy; he jumped around like a puppy.

On the sixth day I learned that Moonstar was taken to the veterinarian to be spayed. Kara Haraden, her husband, and their company, Mohawk Honda, paid for the procedure, as they have for many shelter cats and kittens. Moonstar was also lucky that a human named Wendy Mongillo and her organization called H.O.P.E (Homes for Orphaned Pets Exist) found Moonstar a foster home and put the word out that she needs a forever home. So all my fellow strays had a happy ending to their journey except me. It has been months since I was picked up and while people come looking for pets everyday, I have yet to be chosen.

So during my long days waiting for someone to adopt me, my favorite thing to do was to be walked by a volunteer like Angel Manhardt. Tracy and Cathy organize these volunteers to be sure dogs like me get out regularly for exercise. All the volunteers are very nice. They even contacted Friends of the Saratoga County Animal Shelter to see if they could pay for me to be neutered in hopes that it will make me more adoptable. It worked because soon after I was neutered a tall human came in and asked if he could play with me. I must have made a good impression because he decided to take me home. My chance for a forever home finally came true. So many people at the shelter helped me. They fed me, walked me and helped me look my best. I thank them all and I love my new human. He and I have become best friends.

## Please Leave The Wildlife Alone!!!
(July 17, 2009)

As exciting as it may be to see and hear animals in the wild, it is terribly important to enjoy them from a distance, leaving them to their own adaptive behaviors. For example, feeding wild animals can disrupt their diet and their natural foraging or hunting patterns. It can also make them lose their (healthy) fear of humans and draw them closer to ever encroaching human neighborhoods and developments. An unnatural closeness between humans and wild animals can result in the passing of diseases across species. Rabies is a potentially deadly example of this disease passage from wild animal to human or wild animal to domestic pets.

Rabies is an infectious viral disease that affects the nervous system of humans and other mammals. It has the potential of being lethal if untreated. People get rabies from the saliva, bite, or scratch of an animal with rabies. Wild rabid animals in our area have included sick raccoons, bats, skunks, foxes, and coyotes. These sick animals display unusual behaviors such as extreme aggressiveness or tameness, paralysis, convulsions, excess salivation, difficulty eating or drinking, or unusual vocalizations. Nevertheless, in the early stages of rabies, none of these signs are necessarily apparent.

Animal rabies continues to be a serious problem in New York State. This is especially true in the summer months when people spend more time outdoors and there is increased opportunity for humans and their pets to come in direct contact with wild animals. Pets that have been exposed to rabies, often times by fighting with a rabid animal, can then infect their human owners. More than 35,000 New Yorkers have been treated for exposure to rabies since 1990 and many of these individuals reported contact with a pet that had fought with a rabid animal. Although people usually associate rabies with dogs, among domesticated animals today, rabies is more likely to be found in cats.

Rabies from bats is always a concern. In the past decade, two people in New York State died from bat-associated rabies. In each case, family members recalled a bat in the home; but the possibility of exposure did not occur to them. Bats can lightly scratch or bite a human in their sleep and not be noticed. While 97% of all bats tested by the State Health Department are negative for rabies, New Yorkers should remain aware of the risk for rabies from contact with a bat. It is important to prevent bats from entering occupied spaces in homes, churches, schools, and other similar areas where they might contact people and pets. If you find a bat in your home, do not release or discard it. Immediately contact Saratoga County Public Health at (518) 584-7460.

Pet owners in New York are required by law to have their pets vaccinated for rabies. Sadly, an unvaccinated pet that comes in contact with a rabid or suspected rabid animal must be destroyed or quarantined for six months. In Saratoga County there is no excuse for failing to vaccinate pets when the Saratoga County Animal Shelter (518) 885-4113 regularly holds free vaccination clinics for cats, dogs and domestic ferrets. It is terribly important to keep your pets up-to-date on their vaccinations.

Teaching family members never to handle unfamiliar animals, wild or domestic, even if they appear friendly, can prevent a rabies attack. Remember that signs of rabies are not always obvious especially in the early stages of the disease. When in doubt, err on the side of caution. After exposure, all involved animals should be tested and they should never be handled without heavy protective gloves. If the tests are negative, the treatment will not be necessary. If there is no animal to test, however, because it was discarded or simply not found, treatment should be administered anyway, in case the animal is rabid. To avoid unnecessary rabies treatments, all potentially rabid animals that may have exposed someone should be confined, observed, and tested for rabies by health professionals.

Treatment for rabies should begin as soon as possible after an exposure to a rabid animal. The wound should be thoroughly washed with soap and water. Next the individual should seek a medical treatment called postexposure prophylaxis or PEP. In the United States, PEP consists of one dose of immune globulin and five doses of rabies vaccine over a 28-day period. Rabies immune globulin and the first dose of rabies vaccine should be given as soon as possible after exposure. Additional doses or rabies vaccine should be given on days 3, 7, 14, and 28 after the first vaccination. In the past, this process involved painful injections in the stomach. Current vaccinations are relatively painless and are given in the arm, like a flu or tetanus shot. The good news is there have been no vaccine failures in the United States when PEP was given promptly and appropriately after an exposure to rabies.

Saratoga County Public Health should be contacted immediately when an individual in our area has been exposed to rabies. They are also a good source for updates on the rabies situation and additional information on the disease. To remove stray animals from the neighborhood, residents should call town-affiliated animal control officers. It is also a good idea to have your pets neutered or spayed to help keep them from wandering into habitats of wild animals and of course, to help with the pet overpopulation problem.

For further information on the Saratoga County Animal Shelter, visit www.saratogacountyny.gov or call (518) 885-4113.

If you have any questions concerning wildlife, call the folks at North Country Wild Care. Their number is (518) 964-6740 or visit their website at www.northcountrywildcare.org.

## H.O.P.E., Friends, and the Saratoga County Animal Shelter
(July 24, 2009)

Three years ago I retired after 25 years of teaching anthropology courses at Skidmore College. At first I was pretty miserable without the teaching job I had always loved. But after a time I began volunteer work with FSCAS (Friends of the Saratoga County Animal Shelter). This organization has given me my second career. While helping out I am learning new things about animals, shelters, and animal rescue groups. For example, only recently have I been able to understand the differences and the similarities between FSCAS and another local organization called H.O.P.E. (Homes for Orphaned Pets Exist).

These two non-profits, Friends and H.O.P.E. are both concerned with homeless animals and they both work amicably with our county animal shelter, but each takes a different approach. They do not compete, but rather compliment each other in their efforts to find forever homes for abandoned and lost pets. H.O.P.E. is the older of the two organizations, founded in 2002 by Wendy Mongillo of Wilton, New York. Friends began in 2007 by two women, Sandy Zanone and Pat Casey. Both of these groups are completely run by volunteers who care deeply about animals in our county. So how do these two organizations differ?

To put it simply, Friends is the fundraising arm of the county animal shelter and H.O.P.E. is a rescue group that fosters animals. Friends focuses on ways to improve the present shelter and ways to continue raising funds for the planned new shelter. Friends is dedicated to making our county shelter the best it can be and the first place residents turn for humane animal adoptions and animal reunions with lost pets. In other words, Friends is dedicated to demonstrating what a public shelter can achieve. On the other hand, H.O.P.E. strives to get animals out of the shelter (particularly special needs animals), place them into foster care, and eventually into adoptive forever homes. They are particularly concerned about older animals that have been in the shelter for long periods of time because they are not being adopted. H.O.P.E. often takes animals that for one reason or another do not show well. Another example that reveals a difference between the two organizations is Friends supports sending shelter employees for educational opportunities where they can learn about cutting edge shelters and new ideas for getting shelter animals adopted, while H.O.P.E. takes animals out of the shelter to public adoption clinics held in malls or other places in the community. In short, Friends looks inward at the shelter and H.O.P.E. looks outward from the shelter.

Founders Sandy of Friends and Wendy of H.O.P.E. together attended a weeklong seminar at Best Friends in Utah, to learn more about shelters and animal adoption. Best Friends is the nation's premiere animal sanctuary. Sandy and Wendy also attend each other's fundraising events and meetings. Some individuals belong to both organizations. Both groups have helped pay to neuter or spay animals and pay for other necessary medical procedures. Will these two groups ever join forces? Perhaps after the completion of the new shelter they will consider such a move. But until then they will each do their best to make things better for the lost, abandoned, and abused animals that find themselves in our county shelter. One works to make the shelter experience better (for example, by providing cat beds) and the other takes the animals out of the shelter to adoption clinics, foster homes, and forever homes. If you or members of your family are sincerely looking for some meaningful volunteer work, I can recommend both of these organizations. H.O.P.E. is always looking for foster families and Friends is always looking for volunteers to help with fundraising events. Donations to H.O.P.E., Friends, or the Saratoga County Animal Shelter are always appreciated.

## My Dog Vida and Her Sixth Sense?
(July 31, 2009)

I cannot fool my dog, Vida. She knows when I am sad, afraid, annoyed, or angry, even before I know it myself. At first I thought she must have a sixth sense like those dogs that have been reported acting strangely before an earthquake hits or dogs that somehow get left behind on a family vacation, only to walk for miles cross-country and ending up home. Or how about stories of the dog that knows when dad is returning home from work ten minutes before he comes down the street or turns into the driveway? Is it a sixth sense or is something else going on? I cannot explain the three examples I cite above, but I think I can clarify Vida's "sixth sense" as informed intuition.

One of the primary ways dogs adapt and survive is by carefully studying his or her owner's every move. That is how dogs learn to live with humans. In other words, if they do not study humans, they will have a harder time surviving. From the dog's point of view pleasing humans means an easy dinner, shelter, and even medical care. In my view this is the difference between dogs and cats. Dogs learn to be close and devoted while cats remain independent and when they do not want human attention, they can be aloof. Many cats can take humans or leave them, while dogs have evolved to be largely dependent on them.

Don't get me wrong, I adore both my dog, Vida and my cat, Sully but Vida sticks to me like glue and Sully only gets close when and if he feels like it. I admire both ways of interacting with humans. I also know I am making broad generalizations here and individual dogs and cats may not fit my characterization, but based on my personal experiences with both dogs and cats, this is how I see them. That being said, let me explain about my failed efforts to fool Vida.

Vida has been my service dog for the past nine years. I got her when she was two years old. She had been in training to be a guide dog for the blind, but like so many others, she was released from the program because she was deficient in some area important for guiding the blind. I had been on a wait list for over two years to get a released dog and was delighted when I got the call to come get her. I am in a wheelchair and she quickly learned to walk by my chair, pick up objects out of my reach, and drop them into my lap. She also learned to go everywhere with me. Best of all she made meeting strangers easier because rather than people becoming uncomfortable around me in my wheelchair, Vida becomes the topic of conversation, neutralizes the situation, and puts everyone at ease.

So why should I try to fool Vida? I try to act confident when I go through automatic doors and when I come down my van ramp, but actually both situations cause me to feel anxious and a little fearful. The automatic doors occasionally close before Vida and I are through them and the ramp can be difficult to manage especially if it or my tires are wet. Vida sees right through my efforts to act brave, picks up on my fear and then tries to avoid both situations. She will simply refuse to go through the doors or mount the ramp.

At first I thought she was just being difficult, but then I realized she was getting her cues from me. She reads the subtlest changes in my body language when we face doors or the ramp. I try as hard as I can to be calm and relaxed, but she knows by my slightest tightening grip on the leash or slight changes in the tone of my voice when I say, 'Vida, let's go!" She just looks at me like I've lost my mind. If she could talk I think she'd say, "Are you kidding? That is the door that closes too soon or that ramp isn't safe. Don't you remember what happened a couple of months ago?" When I insist she go through the doors or down the ramp, she runs as if we will be safe if we just go fast enough.

Of course there are other situations where I cannot fool Vida. I cannot get a dog treat into my pocket without her knowing, remembering, and staying, oh so close all day long. Then there is the leash and the keys that I cannot move without her assuming we are going for a walk. I feel very lucky to have such a close relationship with a canine companion. It almost makes living with a disability all right because that is what brought us together.

One of my best memories of Vida is when she came with me to my Skidmore classes. She would lie down by my chair as I delivered my carefully crafted lectures. At the appropriate time, when I started going on too long, she would quietly groan or begin to snore. The students would burst into laughter because they agreed with Vida's assessment of the lecture that was going on and on.

I guess that after nine years together both of us have become experts at reading each other. It is not knowing through a sixth sense, but rather knowing through careful observation of sounds, sights, smells, touches, and in Vida's case, tastes from her occasional licks. Both of us are using our five senses to study one another and then we each act with an informed intuition.

## Sully the Cat Speaks Out
(Aug. 14, 2009)

When I discovered that Jill wrote a whole column about Vida, I was pur-r-r-r-turbed! Not only did she feature Vida, but she also made it sound like dogs study and read their owners while cats are too aloof to notice. Not true! The only difference is cats are subtler about it while dogs put on a big show wagging their tails and acting cute so they can get a biscuit. The truth is cats rule while dogs CAN ONLY drool!!!

Actually, for a dog Vida is OK. She lets me weave in and out of her legs, she shares her water bowl and beds with me, and occasionally when I get into the catnip, tear through the house and bounce on her back, she does not seem to mind. But enough about Vida—let me introduce myself. I am Jill and Steve's cat, Sully. They brought me home from the shelter two years ago. They also call me "twitch," "scrappy," or "Suleiman, the Magnificent." I am a little guy, but I am a tough guy, just the same. I only weigh 7 pounds, can curl up as tight as a young squirrel, but also can stretch out as long and lean as a weasel.

I am a handsome boy with tiger stripes on my back, legs, and tail, and I have leopard spots on my tummy. I have striking markings around my eyes, almost like a human wearing eyeliner. My color is grey with black highlights. I am short-haired but my tail is really long. I am an indoor cat because Jill says indoor cats live, on average over three times as long as outdoor cats. At times I wish I could go outside, but at least our house has lots of windows with ledges for me to sit on while I watch the birds, squirrels, and chipmunks.

One of my favorite activities is playing with Steve. He and I play pretty rough and I love it. He turns me upside down and lifts me high into the air. Jill, on the other hand, plays gently with me, which is nice too, but I prefer the rough and tumble play with Steve. What I do love to do with Jill is ride around the house on her lap while she operates her power wheelchair. We zoom from room to room and I hang tight.

Jill and Steve bought me a scratching post, but it was not high enough for me to fully stretch out. So they had their builder friend, David (also a cat lover) make me a six foot tall climbing tree with two platforms and a piano wire that bounces every time I hit it with my paw or my tail. I never tire of this tall scratching post/climbing tree. It is terrific. Thanks, David.

When I am feeling a little devilish and Steve is snoozing in his easy chair next to my climbing tower, I quietly reach the top platform then spring down to land on his chest. Wow! He wakes with a start, grabbing at the air because at first he doesn't know what hit him. Then he realizes it was me and I run and hide laughing all the way.

I also love to play with a small tinfoil ball. I bat it around like a hockey player. I hide it under the bed or in the closet, but I always find it again. The string game is fun too. Steve and Jill get me batting at the string with a feather tied to it. The stick makes the string and feather dance and I jump and turn until I am dizzy.

Besides all this play, I love to sleep. I will sleep for hours, open my eyes, yawn, and find a new position to sleep some more. Life is good at our house. But never forget that cats are watching their humans too. When Steve packs his bags for a short trip, I know he is going to be gone for a few days and the night before he leaves I curl up next to him with my purring motor going strong because I will miss him. That is not being aloof. So always remember that cats are different from dogs, but just as terrific because cats rule while dogs can only drool!

## Lions and Tigers and Bears, Oh My!
(Aug. 21, 2009)

Why do people in the U.S. and Europe want exotic wild animals for pets? Why are they willing to pay hefty fees for them? Is it the drive to own something most people do not have? Is it a status symbol? If it is a status symbol, it is a very cruel one that is harmful to the animals, harmful to people, and harmful to the environment. The exotic pet trade is also illegal.

If you have the money and access to the Internet, buying exotics is fairly simple. There are plenty of dealers who will find you rare lizards or snakes, cheetahs or black panthers, and monkeys or redheaded Amazon parrots. Nevertheless, these animals suffer terribly in their capture and transport. Most die before they reach their destination and those that make it do not live long in their new environment. Malnutrition, stress, trauma, and behavioral disorders are common in exotics kept as pets. They are not domesticated and people do not know how to care for them.

When an exotic pet becomes ill, it is difficult to find a veterinarian who knows what to do. It will be a challenge to find a vet to treat your pet prairie dog's monkeypox or your bearded dragon's salmonella. Some of the diseases carried by exotic pets are zoonotic—diseases that can be transmitted from wild animas to humans. A few examples include hepatitis, ringworm, tuberculosis, measles, and monkey pox.

Since by definition, wild animals are not domesticated, their behavior may seem unpredictable to humans. There are plenty examples of exotic pets suddenly turning on their trainers, owners, neighbors, or innocent bystanders. These attacks can be horrific and in the end the animal usually pays with his life. For the exotic animals and the people who want them, it is tragic.

Removing animals from their habitat is harmful to the environment, especially when the animal is an endangered species. As their numbers diminish, the ecosystem becomes out of balance. Plants and other animals are affected. Then when they are introduced to a new ecosystem and escape or are let loose by their disillusioned owners, they can again disrupt an ecosystem. Take for example the Nile monitor, native to Africa, but introduced into Cape Coral, Florida. It was sold as an exotic pet, but when it reached its full size, people turned them loose. Residents now claim these large lizards are eating the eggs of burrowing owls, a beloved native endangered species.

The trade in exotic wild animals is a lucrative worldwide industry. According to the ASPCA and the Animal Law Coalition, it generates $25 billion a year. About a quarter to a third of the trade is illegal. Unfortunately, the laws differ from country to country and state to state. Enforcement is difficult because typically raids are spotty and underfunded. For example, the U.S. Fish and Wildlife service only inspects 25% of live animal shipments. At the same time, punishments frequently are little more than a slap on the wrist. Even when there are enforceable laws against the industry, exceptions are made for licensed breeders, dealers, exhibitors, and even operators of auctions.

One of the most disturbing examples of trade in exotic animals involves the poaching of large parrots from the wilds of Mexico and South America. So many of these beautiful and intelligent birds die before they even get to market. To keep them quiet during a smuggling operation, some are drugged or have their beaks taped shut. The demand driving the lucrative trade in parrots is none other than the average American, British or European citizen who want them as pets. As a result, almost a third of the world's parrot species are threatened with extinction.

What can you do about this? Let people know about the tragic side of importing exotic wild animals. Learn more about laws designed to protect animals and organizations like the Animal Law Coalition that advocates for animals "to live free of cruelty and neglect." Do not support pet shops that encourage the sale of exotic animals as pets. And finally, remind people that rather than supporting the exotic animal trade, they need not look further than our local animal shelter for terrific pets. So many cats and dogs are still waiting patiently for their forever loving home.

## More on Cats
(Aug. 28, 2009)

If you read "Sully Speaks Out" a couple of columns back, you know this cat of ours has an attitude, doesn't he? Yesterday he asked me to write my column on the subject of his ancestry. He wanted to know about the origins of the domestic cat. Here it is, Sully:

A modern domestic cat like Sully is most likely a descendant of the African wild cat (Felis sylvestris libyca). The African wild cat still survives in parts of Africa, western Asia, and southern Europe. It is a cat that is relatively social, can be tamed, and frequently lives on the outskirts of human settlements. The African wild cat shares many characteristics with the domestic cat. They are both hunters with amazing pouncing and climbing skills. They also have the same number of chromosomes.

At first early humans probably hunted these wild cats for food and for their pelts. But when human groups began to grow food along with hunting and gathering, they needed to develop ways to store and protect the harvest from invading hungry rodents. The invention of rodent-proof pottery jars provided early humans with a way to safely store foodstuffs, while the cat took the role of rodent exterminator. This domestication of the cat probably occurred 5-8,000 years ago. In contrast, the domestication of the dog occurred some 50,000 years ago to aid in the hunt and to act as beasts of burden. In other words, dogs were domesticated for a nomadic hunting and gathering life, while cats were domesticated for the more sedentary life of early horticulturalists.

By 3500 BC in ancient Egypt cats became much more than rodent killers. Wall paintings in tombs often featured cats as being part of domestic daily life. After the death of a housecat, Egyptian families would ritually mourn. Egyptians saw the cat as a fertility symbol. In ancient Egyptian mythology, Bastet, daughter of the sun god Osiris, and goddess of fertility was first depicted as a lion, but later took the form of a small cat. In 1890 more than 300,000 cat mummies were found in a sanctuary honoring Bastet. There also were mummified mice for the cats to eat on their journey into the afterlife.

The Roman invaders smuggled cats out of Egypt and took them to their northern conquests. Like the Egyptians the Romans considered cats to be sacred. The Greek historian Diodorus recorded an incident involving a Roman charioteer who was stoned to death by an angry mob after he ran over and killed a cat. When the Roman Empire collapsed, the popularity of the cat also fell. Perhaps those who had been conquered by the Romans wanted nothing more to do with them or their symbols and beliefs. Keeping cats was just one more reminder of Roman rule. Freya, the goddess of love had been depicted surrounded by cats, but after the breakdown of the Empire, she became a frightening witch with evil-looking felines at her side. Throughout post-Roman times, Europeans saw the cat as an associate of witches and evil. In Metz, France, hundreds of cats were burned alive because of their supposed association with witchcraft.

During the 1600s the cat found a place of honor once again. The French clergy and royalty kept cats. One French Harpist left a large part of her estate to her cats and their care. By the 1700s cats appeared in Romantic era portraits as pampered companion pets. In the 1800s domestic cats were shown at country fairs in the United States and in England they were presented at Hyde Park's impressive Crystal Palace.

So Sully's ancestors enjoyed periods of popularity as well as periods of persecution, and they were present at many significant times in human history. They were there when humans began to grow their own food. They were there when Egyptian queens gave offerings to a cat image to ensure the birth of an heir. They were also there when Romans invaded Europe. Sully's ancestors were present when Europeans hunted down witches. They were there to pose for a 16th century portrait artist. And finally, Sully's ancestors were present for the first U.S. and British cat showings.

## The Overpopulated World of Pets
(Sept. 4, 2009)

There are too many photos and descriptions of shelter animals that need homes! How can I pick just six for this week's pet page? Chad Beatty, the publisher of *Saratoga Today* said, "I can't believe there are so many homeless animals!" I could only nod my head in agreement and mutter, "yes, doesn't it break your heart?" But now I must decide. I want to include them all, but that would fill page after page. So I am left each week with the difficult choice of picking only six animals to highlight. What can be done to reduce the numbers of unwanted pets? The answer is to convince pet owners to spay or neuter their animals.

There are many reasons to spay or neuter companion pets. First, it helps to reduce pet overpopulation and that will reduce the need for drastic measures like euthanasia. There are simply too many dogs and cats that need families and homes. The surplus of cats is particularly troublesome because cats are 45 times more prolific than humans. I guess the ancient Egyptians knew what they were talking about when they made the cat a fertility symbol. Dogs aren't much better, being 15 times more prolific than humans. The result is too many cats and dogs for the number of humans who can care for them. Dogs and cats do not need help from humans to reproduce, but they do need our help to control their numbers until there are good homes for all of them.

Second, sterilizing your pet can give him or her a longer and healthier life. Canines who are altered live on average 1 to 3 years longer than an unaltered dog. For felines it is 3 to 5 years longer. Animals that have been spayed or neutered have a low to no risk for many types of tumors and cancers. Altered pets are less likely to roam, less likely to be hit by a car, and less likely to be injured or killed during a fight with another animal. For example, bites or scratches from cats fighting over territory or a mate can lead to the spread of Feline Immunodeficiency Syndrome.

Third, according to Spay/USA, a nonprofit organization dedicated to educating pet owners about the benefits of altering their pets, the capture, impoundment and eventual destruction of unwanted animals costs taxpayers and humanitarian organizations over a billion dollars a year. All this could become unnecessary if responsible pet owners have their animals spayed or neutered. So why do some people choose not to alter their pets?

There are some myths that make people hesitate. It is said that animals will get fat because they have been spayed or neutered. This is not true. Pets get fat because they are fed too much and exercised too little. Another myth is that female cats and dogs should have one litter before they are altered. This is not true either. And finally, it is a myth that sterilization will adversely affect their personalities. Again this is not true. There is no evidence to confirm any of these myths. The truth is a neutered pet makes a better pet—one that will not spray on your furniture or bleed on your carpets.

What does it cost to have a pet altered? Fees vary from one veterinarian to another, but if you are struggling economically, there are places where you can apply for help with the cost of spaying/neutering. For example, if you are on public assistance, contact the New York State Department of Agriculture and Markets, Animal Population Control Program at (518) 457-3502 or visit their website at www.agmkt.state.ny.us/ai/apc.html. There are other sources for low cost spay/neuter programs. APF Veterinarians in Scotia has a program with some financial assistance for lower income families, but they must apply for aid in advance. Call for more information (518) 248-0355 or (518) 365-6516. The Cat Care Coalition of Albany also offers low cost sterilization for the pets of individuals with limited funds. Friends of Animals are yet another source for low cost spay/neuters. For more information contact them at (800) 321-7387 or visit info@friendsofanimals.org. A call to your local ASPCA may give you other ideas as well.

Step up and help with the problem of pet overpopulation. Have your pets spayed or neutered because it is good for them, it is good for you, and it is good for our community.

## The Healing Power of Dogs
(Sept. 11, 2009)

Several times a week, Vida and I go visiting at the nursing home where my mom has been for the past four years. These visits are bittersweet, but Vida's presence helps. Years ago she passed her therapy dog test and she has been coming with me to the home ever since. All the residents on mom's floor look forward to seeing Vida. The few times that I left Vida home resulted in disappointed faces and many questions. Where's Vida? Where is the dog? Is she sick? It is humbling to know that Vida is the main attraction, and I am just the woman holding the other end of her leash.

What makes Vida such a wonderful therapy dog? Unlike some therapy dogs, she doesn't climb up on a resident's bed to cuddle with them and she doesn't perform any cute tricks to make them laugh. But what she does do is communicate a powerfully calming influence. This is especially true now at nearly 12 years old. Like most of the residents she too is a senior citizen that has learned from a life of experiences with people.

Vida also seems to have a positive calming effect on the staff. These professional caregivers of the elderly and the infirm are amazing people. They are patient beyond belief and yet there must be times they feel down from the loss of a favorite patient or they feel frustrated by the demands of the families or the many regulations they must follow as they care for the residents. Somehow, even within the difficult job they perform, they will take a moment to marvel at Vida's calming presence.

One resident that always delights in seeing Vida is a woman who suffered a stroke that damaged the speech center of her brain. As a result, after her stroke she never spoke. Nevertheless, she has a very expressive face that would light up when she saw Vida and me coming down the hall. She would wheel her chair toward us and reach out to pet Vida on the head. One day, to everyone's surprise she said in a strong voice, "Nice Dog!" On our next visit, I noticed that while she stroked Vida she began to mumble to herself or to Vida a string of sentences. They were not clear enough for me to understand, but she seemed happy to be conversing anyway.

Another stroke victim on the floor is a man who now has a terrible time with short-term memory. He had to ask nurses repeatedly for their names even though they had been his nurses for months. He was delighted to see Vida and was convinced he was Vida's favorite resident. At first he asked repeatedly about her name, but lately, he has been able to recall her name and has been very excited that he could remember. It clearly gave him a boost to know he remembered her name. He also loved the idea that he was Vida's favorite.

Now, those of you who are regular readers of "Whiskers and Tales" know what happened the last time I devoted my column to Vida. Yes, my cat Sully was "pur-r-r-turbed." So I must remind Sully that way back in March I wrote about the healing power of cats. For Sully's sake I will repeat a segment of that column here:

"Today, the better nursing homes are aware of the benefits of having visiting and resident animals on the premises. Some floors have a cat that is free to roam and others welcome regular visits from licensed therapy dogs. Many of the elderly miss having a cat or dog of their own, and when they can hold or see animals in the nursing home, they can reminisce about a lifetime of animals they once loved and for which they dearly cared. When Douglas' father was seriously ill in a nursing home, the resident cat would not leave his side until he passed. Apparently this was not the first time this same cat was drawn to the side of a dying resident."

In response to this story about cats and dying patients one reader e-mailed me about an article in the New England Journal of Medicine that was devoted to the issue of cats staying by dying patients.

---

## Estherville, A Family Run Animal Sanctuary
(Sept. 25, 2009)

My friend and fellow animal lover, Angel asked me to go with her to visit Estherville, a non-profit, no-kill animal shelter in Greenfield Center. I had never been there before, but I had heard about the place. The name Estherville always made me think of one of those scary movies with an old haunted Victorian mansion up on the hill. In addition, people filled me with images of Estherville as a depressing place. These were the erroneous preconceived ideas I had, but our visit changed all that. I came looking for a frightening, depressing place and I went away with an image of a loving sanctuary where so many animals that others had dismissed as hopeless, find care and hope for adoption. I also came away with a tremendous admiration for the four generations of strong women who have made Estherville a very special place, built on family, love, and a belief in the goodness of animals. But I am getting ahead of myself.

Angel told me she goes to Estherville regularly, bringing them cleaning supplies, pet food, kitty litter, and whatever else they need for the animals. So our first stop before heading out to Greenfield was the dollar store where we got mops and disinfecting solution. Next we stopped at the grocery store for kitty litter and bleach. With these purchases and some large bags of donated dog food we headed out of town to the unpaved gently winding country roads to Estherville. When we arrived there were a couple of volunteer dog walkers with pit bulls that had just returned from their jaunts out to a stream where the dogs could have a quick dip. There also was happiness among the volunteers and employees because two dogs had been adopted that morning.

The history of Estherville begins in the early 1950s when Edna-Ann Klare Senecal and her father Henry Klare began sheltering 48 homeless animals including a horse. There were few funds but they had the support of friends who believed in the cause. As the numbers of animals in need grew, Edna-Ann's father cashed in his government bonds and acquired a 50-acre site in Greenfield Center, where the sanctuary still stands today. In 1954 Estherville received its first charter under the legal name of Estherville, the Alberta and Winonica Memorial Animal Shelter, Inc. The name came from three of Edna-Ann's childhood dogs—Esther, Alberta, and Winonica. In Oct. of 2007 Edna-Ann died at the age of 92. Now Edna-Ann's daughter, Muriel Walter Gurren, her granddaughter, Tracy Gurren Palmateer, her granddaughter's husband, Andrew Palmateer, and her great granddaughters, Jamie, Rosemary, and Angela Palmateer run Estherville.

The site includes four houses for the cats, each with windows and access to a small fenced area so they have both an outside and an inside space. For the dogs, each has their own run, again with both an inside and outside area. There is heat in the winter and AC in the summer for both the cats and the dogs. In addition, there is a small office building and an infirmary. In terms of personnel, at this time there are about 15 volunteer dog walkers and five paid employees. Muriel and Tracy consider them all as part of their family.

Muriel and Tracy sat for a moment and talked with me about their respective projects. Muriel created a thrift shop on the property to raise money. This project has been successful, but the need for garage sale items never ends. On the other hand, Tracy's project began in 1992 when she started taking in cats with AIDS and Leukemia. One of the cat houses is only for cats with AIDS and another is only for cats with Leukemia. Tracy noted that the public is misinformed about both these diseases in cats. One of her cats with Leukemia lived to be 18 years old!

Estherville often helps out when our Saratoga County Animal Shelter is too full. They come and take as many dogs and cats as they can handle. So some of the Saratoga County Animal Shelter cats and dogs end up in Estherville. And that is exactly what happened to Max.

Those of you who have been regular readers of this column will remember Max, the Rottweiler mix I adopted, but after three weeks he attacked my service dog, Vida. I felt I had to take him back to the shelter and later I learned he was adopted again in a few days. Apparently, this second adoption did not work out either because Max messed up again by attacking another dog. When I learned this, I feared Max's days were numbered. But Max was one of the county shelter dogs to be taken in by Estherville. As I talked with Tracy and Muriel I could see Max in his pen. Muriel said one of the dog walkers is working with Max on his dog aggression issues.

There are many things people can do to help out Estherville. Dependable dog walkers are always welcomed as are cash donations. Sheets, blankets, and towels are useful as are mops, cleaning supplies, brooms, rugs, carpet remnants and returnable beverage cans and bottles. Cat litter, cat food, dog food, dog treats, and pet toys are great too. Estherville can also use stamps, note paper and envelopes for the handwritten thank you notes they send people who have helped them and the animals.

Perhaps the biggest need at this time is a replacement for their old van that they use to transport animals and supplies. Another need is for a carpenter to volunteer some time to make repairs. They also really need help with fundraising. Muriel and Tracy are so busy running the place, they have little time for organizing fundraisers or for writing grant applications.

As I sat with Tracy and Muriel, I could hear their 20 roosters crowing. They told me they also have horses, goats, a bull, and a geriatric rabbit that they call the energizer bunny. Both women are strong caring country people who are dedicated to the many animals that end up in their care. They work with Dr. Stiffler, a veterinarian who adjusts his regular fees for Estherville animals.

So the expenses are great—heating, cooling, medicines, food, vet care, and the transportation of animals, while the funding is erratic and meager. I urge people to visit Estherville and find some ways to contribute. Estherville is a non-profit organization and all donations are tax deductible.

If you do pay a visit to Estherville, I hope you get a chance to meet these two remarkable women who are now the backbone of the shelter. Clearly the love of animals and the strength of character to make a difference run in the veins of these four generations of Estherville women. Perhaps one day Muriel and Tracy will see Edna-Ann's dream of a time when there will no longer be a homeless animal problem.

## A Good Dog Is A Trained Dog
(Oct. 2, 2009)

Dogs are capable of learning behaviors that make them into wonderful pets, but they need someone to teach them these behaviors. There are many ways to teach dogs and every trainer believes their way is the best way. Some argue you should reward pets with bits of food during training, others say all you need is a clicker, and still others argue that the dog in training must wear a tight choker. I find that the proper approach depends on the individual dog's drives and temperament. One size does not fit all. Take for example my dog, Vida. Vida has a very high food drive and will do just about anything for a piece of hot dog, cheese, apple or carrot. Vida also is a very sensitive dog that will shut down if a trainer is too heavy handed. She does best with a light touch, soft but firm voice, and treats. In other words, you need to know your dog before deciding on the best approach for training her.

No matter which approach you follow, it is key that you train with confidence and leadership. Cesar Millan (the Dog Whisperer, National Geographic Channel) describes it as being "calm and assertive." This means your body language and your voice should communicate to the dog that you know what you are doing and are deserving of the dog's respect. Training with frustration, anger, impatience, nervousness, or indecision just does not work. Your dog will see right through you and question why she should do what you want her to do. If you are not the leader, your dog will make up her own mind about how she will behave.

Another thing to remember about training is that it is important for some of it to involve other dogs. Training in small groups helps to socialize your dog. In addition, seeing others make mistakes helps everyone in the class to learn. Training in a group can make the lessons seem like a fun adventure for your dog. Some obedience teachers even let all the dogs off lead to play, rumble and interact with each other at the end of class.

I have been thinking about dog training lately because after over a three-year wait, I have been invited to be a student at the Medford, Long Island training center for CCI (Canine Companions for Independence). This will be an intensive two-week training period with a service dog. No, I am not letting go of Vida, but at 12 years old it is time for her to retire. She will live with us as a pet, but after successfully completing the course at the CCI training center, I will be bringing home a new young service dog.

There will be lectures, teamwork with CCI dogs, tests, and more. The people at CCI will select the dog they feel will be a good match for me. After I am paired with a dog he or she will stay with me in my dorm room. These dogs have been trained to help people with disabilities, but during these two weeks I will be taught how to handle one. I think this will be a tremendous learning experience. During my two weeks at the center, I will try to keep up on my column by writing about the experience. I am looking forward to the whole process. I guess the one good thing about being in a wheelchair is this chance to work with one of these special dogs. Furthermore, I look forward to sharing the adventure with my readers.

## Ling, the Chinese Dwarf Hamster
(Oct. 23, 2009)

My friend's granddaughter Sydney kept telling me I should do a column on hamsters. I thought about it, but since I have never had a hamster, I knew I could only do it with Syd's help. So I interviewed Sydney, a nine-year-old fourth grader from Stillwater Elementary School and she set me straight about the world of hamsters. Her comments demonstrated to me that hamsters make a great first pet to teach kids about the wonders and responsibilities of caring for another living creature.

Sydney got the idea for getting a hamster from one of her video games. After she asked several times, her mom agreed to take her to the pet store to find a hamster. They both soon discovered there are different kinds of hamsters with different markings, sizes, and temperaments. The first one she picked out was a biter and she did not like that at all. The sales lady said she should look instead at the Chinese dwarf hamster since they are particularly gentle and do not bite. Sydney found the one she wanted, brought her home and named her Ling. That was over three years ago and Ling is still with Sydney.

The average life expectancy for a hamster is two years, so being three makes Ling pretty special. Sydney says her longevity is due to the fact that she gets hamster vitamins and hamster yogurt treats. In addition, Ling gets fresh water and plenty of exercise running in her wheel. Sometimes she gets the wheel going so fast, it gets ahead of her little legs and tosses her out onto the cage floor. Nevertheless, she jumps up and does it all over again. Another game that gives Ling a thrill is when Syd puts her in a ball and rolls it all over the house. It is also fun, Sydney explains, to let Ling run up her sleeve and down her front only to pop out at Sydney's waist. That must tickle.

Ling is a soft grey with a black stripe down her back. Sydney says she likes to be held, but when out of her cage she must be protected from the other pets in the house. Like all hamsters, Ling is nocturnal. What she does at night while Sydney sleeps is anyone's guess, but I bet Ling keeps watch over the little girl that brought her home three years ago.

## Canine Companions for Independence
(Oct. 30, 2009)

In less than a week I will be heading off to the Northeast Regional Training Center of Canine Companions for Independence (CCI). I am looking forward to the two weeks of intensive training with a CCI dog selected for me. That's right, I won't have a say as to which dog becomes my new assistance dog. The trainers make that determination based on my needs and personality as well as the needs and personality of the dog. There will be ten other students training with me, all hoping to graduate as a skilled handler of the CCI dog that will come home with them.

Canine Companions for Independence was founded in 1975. It is now the largest assistance dog organization in the world. Their motto is "providing exceptional dogs for exceptional people." The first center was established in Santa Rosa, California. Now there is a center in the southwest, southeast, northeast, northwest, and north central regions of the US. The first dog/handler team graduated in 1976. By 2008, 3,000 dog/handler teams had successfully completed the training and graduated from the program.

I applied for participation in CCI over four years ago. Last year I was invited to spend a day at the Northeast Center. I guess they were assessing me as a potential student. Next, a few weeks ago I received a call inviting me to be a student during the first two weeks of November. They said they had a couple of dogs that might make good matches for me. They also said I needed to bring someone with me. I did not have to ask my friend Sandy more than once. She is an animal lover and was very interested to learn more about dog training. I told her we would share a dorm room and that we would be like college roommates.

Candidates for the program include individuals with autism, spinal injuries, muscular dystrophy, cerebral palsy, Parkinson's, multiple sclerosis, or deafness. The dogs appear to be Golden Retrievers and Labrador Retrievers. Tasks they can perform include picking things up and placing them on the handler's lap, getting things out of the way of the handler's wheelchair, opening and closing doors or drawers, turning lights on and off, opening the refrigerator, taking out the desired product, bringing it to the handler, and closing the refrigerator. In addition, they help individuals by making people comfortable around disabilities. The dog takes the focus off the wheelchair or other walking aid and off the physical disability of the handler.

A very important aspect of CCI is the volunteer puppy raiser. They give the future assistance dogs a good start in life. They then give up the puppy when it is ready to begin advanced training. Not all puppies make it to the advanced training period and are released from the program. The puppy raiser or individuals on a wait list for a released CCI dog can then adopt them. This is very similar to what happens with dogs raised to be Seeing Eye dogs. My dog Vida was a released dog from Guiding Eyes for the Blind. Speaking of Vida, do not be concerned that she will feel displaced by this new dog. On the contrary, Vida will be instrumental in helping the new dog fit into our pack. Her calmness will serve as a positive example and her actions will help the new dog learn our routines. Vida will be retired but will still get her daily walks and plenty of love.

## My CCI Class
(Nov. 20, 2009)

While it is always exciting to go on an adventure, it is also great to come home to Saratoga Springs. Many of my regular readers know I spent the last two weeks as a student at the Northeast Regional Training Center of Canine Companions for Independence (CCI). What an amazing experience! I was one of ten students with various disabilities who were invited to train at the center. After the first three days each of us was matched up with a professionally trained companion dog. Throughout the two weeks we worked 8 hours a day learning how to effectively handle the dog that would soon come home with us to be a helper and a faithful companion.

During this very intensive training period the dogs lived with us in our dorm rooms. We heard lectures each day and engaged in group and/or individual practice sessions. There were daily quizzes, homework assignments, a final exam and very little down time. There were five professional dog trainers, who were very demanding. At times it felt like we were in a type of boot camp. As you can imagine there were moments of frustration as well as moments of joyful success. During all this, the ten of us quickly became a tight group. Before the end, we all had gained not only an assistance dog, but also many new friends—people we will never forget.

I am just beginning to sort out all that I learned at CCI, but I plan to devote my next several columns to describing what we learned about dog handling. It will be a real pleasure to share these stories with the readers of *Saratoga Today*. I thought I would begin by printing the graduation speech that I wrote for the group...

> The CCI fall class of 2009 all agrees that this experience, this very special gift, has been an amazing event in our lives. I describe it as a "moment of time, out of time." What I mean by this is that these two weeks of working and living with these marvelous dogs seemed like a period when ordinary time stood still. And in that space of "time out of time" we could focus entirely on the one task—bringing these animals into our lives to help us cope with each of our personal challenges. Some of us have children with special needs. Others of us have had our adult lives interrupted by challenging illnesses. What we all have in common is the will to live life to the fullest and to do so with love and personal strength. But now we have a four-legged helping partner to accompany us on our life's journey.

During our time at CCI we found encouragement and guidance from a dedicated staff and highly skilled trainers. We also found among ourselves new friendships that we will never forget. We cheered each other on and helped each other out. We heard each other's stories but there was no pity, only admiration. We each thought we were given the smartest, the sweetest, or simply the best dog and we all agreed our trainers knew what they were doing when they matched us up with our canine companions.

We all wrote a bit about how our two weeks of training with our CCI dog has already changed us. Here are a few excerpts from our personal essays:

For someone who has never had a dog before, this has been an amazing experience. In addition to my initial bonding with our CCI dog, Thea, it has been touching to see my son, Benjamin cuddling with "his dog" and taking the responsibility of feeding and brushing him. He has even promised not to open the car door prematurely and give the command "release!" Lana Oresky

My son Marky has improved beyond my expectations. I can only imagine what it will be like as the months pass. The constant drone he makes while riding in the car has turned into giggles and laughter. He is a happier boy because of our CCI dog, Ivory. What a beautiful experience for me to see this change in him. Mark DeMarzio

Brandon was born healthy but at 13 months he was given a medication that caused muscle and brain damage. He is a sweet kid who loves animals so much that sometimes when the dogs are playing in the CCI yard, he thinks they are getting hurt and he cries. Brandon's father and I must fight for his equipment, his therapies, and more. With CCI, however, all we had to do was accept a tremendous gift. Our CCI dog, Elizabeth is going to change Brandon's life. Brandon will always have a friend. Dogs love unconditionally and Elizabeth will be in Brandon's heart forever. Alicia Judd

We also wrote about some funny moments at CCI. For example, pretty little Clare who at first was afraid of the dogs coming too close was soon seen in the play yard smiling, squealing and laughing when a herd of dogs came flying by her almost knocking her over in her wheelchair. And we won't soon forget how Brandon flirted with the CCI photographer, Jennifer, by pulling his hood over his head and peeking out to see her in the lunchroom. Hillary also made us all smile as she danced across the floor in her miniskirt, black tights and boots. Then there was me getting lost every time while driving to our field trip locations. We also enjoyed how David's CCI dog, Kinsel, had a tail that wagged in tight circles like a helicopter ready to lift off the ground. It was also classic when Nancy's CCI dog, Monty peed in the ladies department of Macy's. Finally, most of us learned with envy that soon Brittney's CCI dog, Shawnee will soon join the snowbirds migrating to Florida with her new family every winter.

To close, I would like to read a short poem that Nancy shared with the rest of us in the Fall 2009 graduating class:

*He is your friend, your defender, your dog.*
*You are his life, his love, his leader.*
*He will be yours, faithful and true to the last beat of his heart.*
*You owe it to him to be worthy of such devotion.*

There was hardly a dry eye in the audience at graduation. It was a tremendously moving occasion. My new dog is a male lab and Golden mix named Moses II. Next week I will write more about him and more about the CCI team training. Happy Thanksgiving!

## Moses and Our Pack
(Nov. 25, 2009)

I have been home now for a week since my "boot camp" experience at Canine Companions for Independence. Moses and the other dogs presented to us there were already trained, but we humans had to learn how to get them to do things for us. Many times during our classroom practice sessions, I would mess up an exercise while Moses would look up at me as if to say, "Hey, you should know that by now! Watch me and maybe you will finally get it!" It was humbling, but there was no question that Moses knew what he was doing long before I did. Nonetheless, Moses had tremendous patience and faith that I would get it before long.

After our graduation, (yes, I made it with considerable help from Moses) my first concern was how he would fit into our pack once we got him home. Would Moses, Vida and Sully all get along? Vida is my 12-year-old lab that deserves to retire after ten years as my loyal service dog and Sully is our first cat. Now there also is a second cat that I adopted last October. Her name is Magic. She is all black and very beautiful but not as social as Sully. Anyway, it was very important to me that I set up a positive greeting between these creatures so we can all live in harmony. It took some planning, but things got off to a very good start.

My husband Steve planned to come to our CCI graduation. He took Vida to stay with our friend Pat who has two labs of her own. So Vida had two days with Pat and her dogs. This meant lots of playtime for the old girl. Then an hour before we were to arrive home with Moses, Pat brought Vida back to our house. After we arrived I left Moses in the car while I went in to greet Vida. She was tired from all the play with Pat's dogs but she was happy to see me. Remember a tired dog is a good dog. Next I went back to the car to get Moses.

I brought Moses around to our deck and Steve brought Vida out there too. Moses and Vida met without any growls, barks, or raised hackles. It could not have gone better. Making sure Vida was tired and happy and having them meet out on the deck prevented any displays of jealousy, domination, or aggression over toys or food.

Next Moses had to meet Sully and Magic. Again things went very well. There was no hissing or scratching. I left the leash on Moses just in case, but there were no negative interactions from Moses, Vida, or the cats. Some of this success was a result of planning well, but much of it comes from the calm natures of Vida, Moses, Sully, and Magic. They are all affectionate and non-confrontational creatures.

In addition to his calm and non-confrontational nature, Moses is a very handsome boy. His mother was half Labrador Retriever and half Golden Retriever. His father was pure lab. CCI has been cross-breeding lab and Golden Retrievers because they find they can better avoid health problems associated with each breed and they say the labs bring high intelligence while the goldens bring the calm character. They also claim with the mix they can get a softer coat rather the typically course lab coat.

From his trainers and puppy raisers I learned that Moses loves to swim, play fetch with tennis balls or sticks, and is a very affection guy that loves a tummy rub. Steve and I already feel very lucky to have Moses as part of our pack of critters.

Next week I will write more about the actual training techniques taught to CCI students and dogs like Moses.

## Training at Canine Companions for Independence
(Dec. 4, 2009)

Just as I promised in my last column, today I will share more about the actual training Moses and I received at the Northeast CCI Training Center located on Long Island. One of the first things we learned was how to properly care for our assistance dog. We were shown how to brush his teeth with liver flavored tooth paste, brush his coat, check to see if his nails needed trimming, how to trim his nails when needed, and how to check him over for any potential health problems. This grooming process we were to do every day. In addition, we were to be sure the dog gets at least 1 hour of exercise each day and at least 10-15 minutes of training each day so they will not forget what they already know or to introduce them to a new command.

Moses and the other dogs in our group knew forty-six one-word commands. These commands were to be given firmly and clearly. We were never supposed to give a command more than once, and we were never to gesture along with the verbal cue. If the dog did not respond to the command, we were to give a quick but firm correction with the leash and prong collar. The theory behind this form of training dogs is based on the notion that the dog will not repeat behavior that results in discomfort, but will instead repeat behavior that results in something pleasant. In other words, when the dog ignores a command he gets the discomfort of the prong collar, but when he responds properly we were taught to pour on the praise. We never rewarded with food, but rather enthusiastic admiration. The trainers told us often, CCI dogs work for praise, not food.

I must admit that when we were instructed to use a prong collar I was troubled. I had always associated prong collars with dogs that were really out of control. Why were they telling us to use them on these beautifully trained and very gentle dogs? The trainers responded to my concerns by explaining that the prong collar is more humane than a regular choke collar because it evenly distributes the pressure on the neck. Furthermore, the prong collar is similar to a nip that a mother dog would give to her misbehaving pup. I am still apprehensive about the prong collar, but I told myself when I agreed to come to CCI that I would withhold judgment and be open to trying the training their way.

The forty-six one-word commands that the dogs already knew could be combined for more complicated behaviors. For example, CCI dogs know "up," "get," "hold," "give," and "off." Together these commands can work wonders in a store. When I took Moses into a Cumberland Farms store, my arms were full of items I needed to purchase. Before reaching the counter I decided this would be a good time to put Moses to the test in the "real world." When we got to the counter I told him "up" and he put his front paws on the counter. Then I passed him a $20.00 bill and I said, "get." He took it in his mouth and I said, "hold." Next I told the clerk to hold out her hand and I commanded "give" and Moses let go of the bill and the clerk took it. To conclude, I said, "off" and Moses got his paws off the counter and sat waiting for the next command with his tail enthusiastically wagging or actually sweeping the floor.

When Moses is not working, which he knows is when he doesn't have on his CCI vest and the prong collar, he plays like any other dog. He loves to play fetch with the ball or with sticks. Nevertheless, he seems to get pleasure from working as well. It is almost as if he needs a job and the praise it brings him when he gets it right.

Next week will be my final column in this series on our CCI experience. In it I will discuss the role of the puppy raisers. These are people who have the future CCI dogs for the first year and a half, before turning them over to the trainers. These individuals give up the dogs they have grown to love because they want him to become a service dog that will help someone with disabilities. They start the whole process by setting a foundation for the training and getting the young dogs used to all kinds of different situations that they might encounter later as a service dog. Only about 1/3 of the dogs that start out on this path actually make it to graduation, paired with a disabled individual. If they do not make it to the last steps, the puppy raiser can keep the dog as a pet. Nevertheless, puppy raisers will tell you that having one of their pups make it to graduation is the greatest accomplishment of all. At graduation I got to meet Moses' puppy raiser and I will tell all about that next week too.

## Puppy Raisers, Unsung Heroes In the Making of an Assistance Dog
(Dec. 11, 2009)

At our Nov. graduation from Canine Companions for Independence, my new assistance dog, Moses got to see his puppy raiser once again and I got to meet her for the first time. Puppy raisers are very important individuals in the early life of a CCI assistance dog. They take the CCI puppy into their home for the first year and a half of his life. They are volunteers who teach the dog basic manners, enroll him in a CCI approved obedience course, provide funds for his food, medical, and transportation expenses, and expose him to all kinds of situations for socialization. These socialization situations might include an afternoon at the Mall, a ride on a bus, a hike in the mountains, or a trip to the veterinarian's office. In other words, puppy raisers set the foundations for the dog to become a calm, confident, and obedient canine companion that will be comfortable in a wide variety of situations.

Moses' puppy raiser was a young woman named Bethany. She and her mother have raised several puppies for CCI. Bethany and I will forever be connected by our love and admiration for Moses. At graduation Bethany presented me with a book she made of Moses' puppy pictures. She also told me about his habits, likes and dislikes. That was how I first learned that Moses loves to swim. This was important information since I planned to take him regularly with me to the pool at our YMCA. While Vida, his predecessor never cared much about swimming; I have to be careful Moses doesn't try to jump in and join all the morning swimmers! It also means that once summer comes, Moses and I will be taking trips to local lakes so he can swim too.

CCI puppy raisers are a special group of people. They are always asked how they can give up the dog after a year and a half. Bethany's response is, "It is like sending your children to college. While you are sad to see them go, you don't want them to flunk out and come home. You want them to be successful and graduate." In fact only about 30% of the puppies make it all the way to advanced training and are matched with an individual who needs their skills and companionship. The other 70% are released from the program because of medical reasons (all must pass heart, eyes, hips, and elbow standards), undesirable personality traits such as fearfulness or nervousness in new situations, and finally some are released because the dog doesn't enjoy the work of an assistance dog. Dogs that are released from the program may be adopted by the puppy raiser or may be redirected into another type of work such as search and rescue or police work.

I asked Bethany about families with children that raise puppies. How do the children handle giving up the dog after 18 months? Bethany explained, "Kids and CCI go great together because children run, scream, and do strange things. This is all-important for CCI puppy socialization. But more importantly the kids learn about volunteerism, disabilities, and giving up something important to them in order to help someone else. When Bethany talks to children about CCI, she does her tennis ball demonstration. She has the children sit on the floor and asks one to toss a tennis ball. Next she asks them how they are going to get the ball back if they can't stand up and walk or run to get it. Then she has her puppy in training retrieve the ball. This helps the children understand the concept of a service dog as well as understanding something about what they take for granted—full use of their arms and legs. Nevertheless, Bethany admits that puppy raising is not for all families or individuals because for some the emotional toll is just too much even if the dog makes it all the way to graduation. But for most of the 1,000 CCI puppy raisers the benefits outweigh the hardships. Many pick up their new puppy as soon as they drop off the one they have finished raising.

This wraps up my series of columns on our CCI experience. For those of you who worry about Vida, be assured that she and Moses get along beautifully, Vida is always fed before Moses, and Vida always gets a leisurely afternoon walk. Retirement agrees with her. In dog years Vida is now 84 years old. I also want to say that my concerns about the prong collar are no more. Moses shows me everyday that this tool worked so well in his training that I barely need to touch the leash and he responds.

Finally, I have one last note. With Vida as she neared retirement, I let everyone pet her, but now with Moses, I need to stick more clearly with the "Please do not pet a service dog rule." This is especially true at the YMCA because Moses really has to concentrate on his job there and not his desire to jump into the pool. So if you ask to pet Moses and I say "please don't," do not be offended but remember that by ignoring him it will only make his job easier. Thanks and next week I will write about some of the dangers for cats and dogs around the winter holidays.

## Happy Holidays, But Remember There are Dangers for Pets
(Dec. 18, 2009)

There are plenty of dangers for pets at this time of year. Veterinarians see animals with lacerations from broken ornaments, with lethargy and vomiting after ingesting tinsel, or with pancreatitis after eating too much rich holiday food. It is not a bad idea to find out which emergency animal hospitals will be open over the holidays and tape the phone number to your refrigerator just in case an emergency arises.

There are several plants that we associate with the holidays that can be toxic to pets. The leaves and berries of holly, ivy, mistletoe, balsam, juniper, cedar, pine, fir, lilies, and poinsettias are all in this category. If you use these plants to decorate your home be sure to supervise your pets in these rooms. When you must be gone from your home, leave your pets in a safe room with water and toys.

The Christmas tree itself can also be a problem. Cats love to climb and a Christmas tree full of shiny ornaments, ribbons, and lights will be a great temptation. The tree should be carefully anchored so it will not fall over on a pet. In the line to explain the nature of the emergency. Nonetheless, they decided to check out the situation. The mystery was solved when Rosheisen explained that he always leaves the phone on the floor in the living room and once he tried to train his cat to hit the emergency button on the phone. He never thought the lesson stuck until that day he fell out of his chair. His cat Tommy hit the emergency button and in doing so, he alerted the police. Who says cats can't be trained?

Another cat, famous for her courage during WW II, was a tabby named Faith. Faith was a stray that settled in the Rectory house of London's St. Augustine Church. In 1940 Faith had kittens. The Rector that cared for Faith took the kittens in a basket upstairs for safety. Nevertheless, Faith had other ideas and every time the Rector took the kittens upstairs, Faith would move them again down three flights. Three nights later the blitz began and the Rectory was bombed and burned to the ground. Faith and her kittens were found alive and safe in the rubble. Had they been upstairs they most likely would not have survived.

A 10-year-old cat named Libby of Middleburg, Pennsylvania took charge when her canine housemate, Cashew needed help. Cashew was a senior yellow Lab/Shar Pei that had become blind and deaf. Libby became Cashew's guide. She would herd him toward his food or water and block him from running into obstacles. In 2008 the ASPCA awarded Libby with an award for her actions.

Another example of cat heroics involves an Indiana family that came close to being overcome by carbon monoxide. The Keesling family was asleep when their cat Winnie jumped on Mrs. Keesling and began clawing at her hair until she woke up. Mrs. Keesling realized something was wrong, got her family and cat out of the house, and called for help.

Turning now to dogs, I found many stories of canine bravery and rescue. Dogs have pulled their humans from car wrecks, freezing water, and burning houses. But that is

Vida

Sully

Moses

Magic

Jesse

not all. For example, a Maryland woman, Debbie Parkhurst stretched out for a rest and began to choke on an apple. She gasped for air and felt like she was going to die. Her 2 year old Golden Retriever Toby came to the rescue. He jumped hard on her chest and the piece of apple flew out. Toby's quick action and his version of the Heimlich maneuver saved Parkhurst's life and earned him an award from the ASPCA in 2007.

In 2002 a mixed breed named Foxy walked with her owner every evening. One day after dinner the owner tripped, fell and broke her hip. No one came for over an hour. It wasn't until the dog began barking and howling that someone heard the commotion and came to find the woman in great pain and unable to get up.

Shana, a German Shepherd mix, saved his human family in 2006 when a terrible storm took down many large trees and blocked the only way to safety. Shana dug a tunnel for the family to get to out of danger.

After the destruction of the World Trade Center, a police dog named Trakr searched the rubble and found the last known survivor. Trakr and his human handler were honored for their work and dedication.

My final canine example is Moti, a five-year-old German Shepherd that saved his human family from armed robbers who entered the home. Moti distracted the robbers from harming the family. He was shot for his trouble, but he survived the bullet.

dog's toes and pads. This fur should be kept short so snow doesn't lodge there and cause ice balls to form, annoying or even hurting the dog.

When you really cannot take your dog for a walk due to extreme cold, it is important to come up with other ways to give her exercise. Games like fetch and retrieve can be played in the house with a cloth Frisbee or a cloth ball. After I taught Moses to fetch, I found he will do this forever. He never seems to tire of the game. Finally if you still want to take the dog out for a walk in the bitter cold you should shorten the length of your regular walk.

Two other notes—Be careful your pet doesn't get into the sweet, but highly toxic antifreeze that may be on your driveway or in the road. Furthermore, when it comes to outdoor cats, bring them in when it is very cold and remember that cats sometimes seek shelter and warmth in a car engine. Before starting your car, bang on the hood to give a sleeping cat a chance to escape. Sadly they can be injured or killed by a fan belt.

## Dementia in Dogs and Cats
(Jan. 29, 2010)

The other day it became painfully clear that my 12-year-old black lab, Vida, has cognitive dysfunction syndrome (CDS), or a cluster of symptoms that can indicate dementia. I took both Vida and Moses to be photographed by Mark Bolles at his Geyser Road photo studio. My husband Steve gave me a gift certificate last Christmas for Mark to make a portrait of the two dogs together. Setting up for the shoot was hard because Vida seemed to forget the most basic commands like sit, stay, and down. These are all commands that she has known for years, and yet she just looked at Mark and me with confusion.

In the past year I have noticed some other strange behaviors from Vida. She stands by the back door until I let her out into our fenced yard. I watch her from our kitchen window as she slowly makes her way to my wheelchair ramp that takes her off the deck and into the yard. There are steps too, but she stopped using them several months ago. Once out in the yard, Vida seems to be in a daze, unsure of what to do next. Sometimes she simply wanders, looks disoriented and then makes her way back to the door and stands there waiting to get back into the house. When I open the door to let her in, she hesitates and then runs in as if she is not sure she will make it without the door closing on her. Some of my readers might remember how a couple of months ago, I wrote that Vida was acting nervous about getting into my van or getting through open doors. At the time, I thought she was simply picking up my nervousness about getting my wheelchair into the van or through automatic doors, but now I think these behaviors were all probably tied to canine dementia.

Dogs, cats, and their humans are all, on average living longer. This longevity in dogs and cats is due to improved nutrition, veterinary care, and better-educated owners. With longer lives dogs, cats, and humans are getting more old age diseases such as dementia, arthritis, and hypertension. This column begins a three-part series on the aging process in our pets. This first installment focuses on dementia in senior canines and senior felines. What is dementia and is it common for pets to have it? What are some signs that your pet might have dementia? At what age can dementia be discovered? Finally, what can an owner do for a pet with dementia?

Dementia is mental deterioration in the elderly. It involves a progressive deterioration of memory, spatial orientation, and temporal recognition. Dementia is sometimes referred to as "senility" or "Alzheimer's disease." Millions of dogs and cats have dementia in their senior years. There are some warning signs for dementia:

- Spatial disorientation or confusion. A cat might forget where the litter box is or a dog might feel trapped in a corner of a room. Some dogs with dementia will face a wall and stare into space.
- Altered relationships with their human or other animals in the house. A pet might not recognize his owner or the other animals in the house.
- Increased anxiety. A cat might suddenly become anxious about another cat he used to play with or a dog with which he used to sleep.
- Changes in sleeping pattern. The time of day or the length of a nap may be altered so the animal can sleep longer or more frequently.
- Inappropriate vocalizations. A dog may suddenly bark in the middle of the night for no apparent reason.
- Loss of memory. The pet may forget commands or even toileting rules.
- Changes in activity. A cat may lose interest in playing with a favorite toy.
- Lack of interest in food. A dog or cat might turn up their noses at food that previously had been enthusiastically eaten.
- Decrease in grooming. A cat no longer grooms himself.
- Confusion about the passage of time. A dog forgets he was already walked.

If your dog or cat displays several of these behaviors, he might have dementia and you should consult your vet.

Determining when your pet could be considered a senior depends on his size and breed. For dogs, the smaller breeds generally live longer than the large breeds. In addition, on average mixed breeds live longer than purebred dogs. For cats, they can be considered geriatric between 8 and 12 years old. Siamese cats tend to live longer and Persians have shorter life spans. Aging is not a disease. It is a natural process, but it can pave the way for cognition diseases like dementia.

Understanding the normal aging process in dogs and cats can help to identify any unusual illnesses. The normal aging process involves a general slowing down, graying around the face and muzzle, hearing loss, muscle atrophy, and cloudy or bluish eyes. This change in the eyes can occur in geriatric dogs or cats. It is not the same as cataracts that can adversely affect vision. The cloudy or bluish eyes do not affect the animal's ability to see.

Dogs and cats with dementia can still enjoy life. Treatment might include food rich in antioxidants and vitamins, a stimulating environment with plenty of human/pet interactive playtime, and there are medications that you might consider in consultation with your veterinarian. It may also be helpful for a pet with dementia to have a quiet place somewhere in the house that promises peace and safety. Next week I will continue exploring the aging process in pets with a closer look at arthritis in senior dogs and cats.

## Oh My Aching Back! Arthritis In Older Dogs and Cats
(Feb. 5, 2010)

Aging in dogs and cats is the topic of this three part series. Last week in part I, I looked at dementia in older dogs and cats and this week I am turning to arthritis in elderly pets.

Arthritis is an inflammation of the joints that can affect pets and pet owners alike. In humans it is most often associated with infectious or autoimmune causes. In pets it is more frequently due to developmental degenerative disease or by direct injury to a joint. This is more common in elderly dogs and cats because their longevity has given them more opportunities for an injury that could result in arthritis. It is also found more often in overweight pets because they are putting more weight on their joints.

The most common direct causes of arthritis in pets are hip or elbow dysplasia. These conditions are found most often in large, fast-growing dogs. Nevertheless, arthritis does occur in smaller dogs and cats as well. Healthy joints are made up of cartilage and soft connective tissue providing smooth movement and absorbing the shock of a hard landing. When this cushion of cartilage and soft tissue takes a beating from activities, it becomes inflamed and painful. When I see my 12 year old lab, Vida get up from a nap, it is easy to see that she is feeling pain in her hips. Other things to watch for are lameness, stiffness, trouble navigating stairs, hesitation before jumping, falling on slippery floors, difficulty getting comfortable, or being restless at night.

Pets with arthritis can be given an anti-inflammatory drug such as buffered aspirin. Never assume that you can guess at how much to give your pet. Always consult your veterinarian first because many anti-inflammatory drugs given at the recommended level for humans will be toxic in pets.

Light exercise is helpful for an arthritic pet. Swimming is probably the best form of exercise but finding a place for your pet to swim is not easy especially in the middle of a nasty New York winter. Some vet offices actually have tubs for exercising a dog with arthritic pain.

Once the pain has been addressed with the proper dose of an anti-inflammation drug, the animal's weight needs to be carefully monitored. The heavier the animal, the more stress is placed on those joints. Just one more reason to be sure your pet does not become overweight. In very severe cases there are some surgical procedures that can be explored with your vet. In some cases a total hip replacement or the removal of bone and cartilage fragments may be in order.,

## Hyperthyroidism, Hypertension, & Heart Disease
(Feb. 12, 2010)

Poor little Vida! Ever since I started writing about geriatric health issues for dogs and cats, she has endured my concerns and probes as I worry she might be a victim of dementia, arthritis, and now hyperthyroidism, hypertension, and heart disease. Actually Vida is very healthy at 12-years old. Nevertheless, when I research a medical condition, I suddenly see evidence that she might have the disease. I guess I am becoming a hypochondriac for my dog!

The good thing about this is that I am paying closer attention to the health of Vida and Moses. One thing I have noticed since Moses has settled in is Vida has gained confidence through him. He goes through doors without hesitation, jumps into the van without hesitation and she just follows him. Moses is helping the old gal with her fears and phobias. It is heartwarming to see a younger dog helping an older one. She even jumps up to walk with Moses and me when in the past she showed little interest. I really think Moses has given Vida a new lease on life. So lets turn now to the topics on this third column in the series: hyperthyroidism, hypertension, and heart disease.

The thyroid gland produces hormones that regulate many vital body functions. Tumors of the thyroid gland will cause an overproduction of these hormones or hyperthyroidism. In cats the tumors are typically benign and do not spread to other organs. In dogs these tumors are more frequently malignant and will spread throughout the body. Signs of hyperthyroidism include weight loss even with an increased appetite, increased water intake, frequent stools, restlessness, and panting. For canine hyperthyroidism, surgical removal of the tumors is usually recommended because pre-cancerous cells may be present.

An overactive thyroid (hyper-) speeds up the metabolism and body processes while an underactive thyroid (hypo-) forces everything to slow down. Both conditions can be found in dogs and cats, but dogs age two or older are more likely to develop hypothyroidism and middle-aged and older cats are more likely to develop hyperthyroidism. To determine either hyper- or hypo- thyroid conditions, a blood test is administered and changes in weight, appetite, behavior and appearance give clues to a diagnosis. Medication to correct the problem should be discussed with your veterinarian.

Thyroid troubles can contribute to high blood pressure (hypertension) in dogs and cats. In dogs and cats this condition is typically found when other diseases such as kidney disease or heart disease are also present. As you can imagine, taking blood pressure in Fluffy or Fido is no easy task. A cuff must be placed on the animal's leg or tail before blood pressure can be measured. Several readings should be obtained and averaged since like people, stress of the situation will show increased levels of blood pressure and once the animal or human calms down, blood pressure drops. Treatment for high blood pressure in dogs or cats typically involves medicines designed to lower blood pressure. It also might involve treating the other medical conditions that are underlying or causing the high blood pressure.

One of those underlying conditions may be a form of heart disease. Dogs and cats can be born with a defective heart or they can develop problems over time. For example, the heart may become enlarged and the result may be congestive heart failure. In dogs, scarring from heart valve problems may also result in a failure of the heart to promote healthy circulation. To treat these problems there are many medications developed for humans with heart disease that can be adjusted for a cat or dog. Again, consult your vet.

This completes my three-part series on health problems of senior cats and dogs. May you and your pets enjoy wellness in 2010!

## Establishing a Strong Bond Between You and Your Pet: The Importance of Regular Grooming
(Feb. 19, 2010)

Grooming involves the power of touch. Just stroking a dog or cat can lower the blood pressure of a human, and it can also lower the blood pressure of the dog. In other words, grooming can be a positive experience for both human and pet. Did you know that Cesar Millan, the "Dog Whisperer" began his career as a dog groomer?

The best way to establish a positive foundation of touch is by giving your pet a regular grooming schedule. This gives structure to your pet's experience with being touched. A confident calming touch builds trust while rough handling can erode that trust. Furthermore, well-groomed pets get more cuddles because they are clean and smell nice. But there are other benefits as well.

While regularly grooming your pet, you might notice changes that could mean health issues. For example, a human who brushes his dog regularly could notice a lump that should be checked out by the veterinarian. Early detection could make all the difference in the dog's future. Daily grooming at home should include brushing the coat and the teeth, cleaning the ears, periodically trimming the nails, and giving a once over to check for any concerning changes in the eyes, skin, and paw pads.

Brushing teeth and trimming nails are not as easy as brushing the coat. For teeth and nails you can get advice from your vet or you can let a professional groomer perform these tasks. I have never had great luck with brushing my pets' teeth or trimming the nails. For the teeth brushing I bought liver flavored toothpaste from the pet shop, but all Moses and Vida want to do is lick the liver paste off the brush before I can get started. I also have never tried to brush the cat's teeth. With the nail trimming, I am always too afraid of cutting them too close to the quick and causing pain for the dogs or cats. Nevertheless, I know plenty of pet owners who do these grooming tasks themselves.

Some breeds need more grooming than others. The longhaired dogs and cats get tangles that can mat and create skin sores. This may require a visit to a professional groomer. Pets that go to the groomer regularly often learn to enjoy the experience. Those that rarely go tend to find the experience frightening or painful. Shorthaired pets need less grooming but it is still important that their skin oils are distributed throughout the coat, loose hair needs to be removed, and ears, teeth, and nails need to be checked.

Watching a skilled professional groomer at work is a learning experience. They develop a calm assertive touch when they work with many different breeds and personalities. Pet owners can learn to be calm and assertive as they groom their dogs and cats. This will only enhance the bond between them and their pet. If your pet starts off resisting your efforts to groom, be patient and the animal will learn to love these times with you. In order to live in close contact with humans, dogs and cats need conditioning to human touch. Grooming is the way to provide this conditioning.

## The World According to Moses
(Feb. 26, 2010)

Jill has been writing all the pet columns lately. She does a pretty good job for a human, but wouldn't you rather get a dog's point of view now and then? I think it is high time for Jill's readers to hear from me, Moses II.

I am the newest member of Jill's pack. I am two years old and they say I am a very handsome boy. My mother was half Golden Retriever and half Labrador. My father was all Labrador. My trainers say my smarts come from my Lab father and my sweetness comes from my half Golden mother. Does that make me one of those designer dogs like a Labradoodle? I hope not because I was bred to be a CCI dog (Canine Companions for Independence). I am proud to wear my blue and yellow vest with the picture of a dog sitting by a person in a wheelchair. CCI dogs like me train for two years to become a helper to people like Jill—people with disabilities. For example, when Jill drops something like her keys in the snow, I pick them up on command and place them gently on her lap. I also keep her company because her husband Steve is off to work all the time. Furthermore, I help Jill by giving people something other than her wheelchair on which to focus.

Jill's pack consists of Steve, Vida, Sully, Magic, and me, Moses. Steve and Jill, as human husband and wife are our co-pack leaders, Sully and Magic are cats, and Vida and I are the canines of the group. Let me tell you about each member of our pack from my perspective.

Vida (pronounced VEEDA) is a sweet old gal. Her name means "life" in Spanish. Jill named her that because after she adopted Vida, she felt like the dog helped her recover and regain life from a period when she was pretty sick and in the hospital. But that was a long time ago. Vida is now a 12 year old Black Lab with some grey around the muzzle. Lately Vida seems to get confused about things. For example, she is afraid to go outside because she worries that the door will close on her. It seems like some sort of phobia. But that is where I come in because I go out the door first and show her there is nothing to fear. She picks up on my confidence and just follows me out. She also complains about her aches and pains especially when she gets up after a nap. I do not know what to do about that, but Jill learned from our veterinarian that she could safely give Vida one aspirin every 12 hours. It seems to work because after she swallows the pill, she stops complaining for a while. The only thing I do not like about Vida is that she never wants to play with me. She just wants to eat, sleep, and go for her daily walk with Jill.

Now then, Sully is a very friendly tabby cat. Jill adopted him from the shelter when he was just a kitten. He is grown up now and will come up to me and put a paw on my shoulder or weave in and out my legs. He has also been known to chase my tail or my leash when Jill is trying to get me ready for a walk. Actually he has become my playmate since Vida won't play. I do not mind except that Sully can only play inside. Jill will not let him outside because she says most outdoor cats do not live as long with all the dangers outside—dangers like cars, dogs, wild animals, and kids who never learned to be kind to animals. The best way for me to describe Sully is to compare him to a clown, always acting silly, happy, and funny. He makes Jill and Steve laugh at his antics all the time.

Finally there is Magic, the black cat that Jill adopted from the rescue group, H.O.P.E. (Homes for Orphaned

Pets Exist). Magic was a two-year-old homeless girl. She had been in three different foster homes, but still needed a forever home. Kittens get adopted all the time, but older cats are often passed over because they are not as "cute" as a kitten. Nevertheless, Jill saw something special about Magic. Soon after this black cat joined the pack, she became very attached to Steve. She follows him around the house like a dog and likes to perch on Steve's stomach as he sleeps. Magic is very beautiful with eyes that change hue from yellow to green to a deep blue depending on the light.

Well, this has been fun. Maybe Jill will let me write the column again some time. Before I close, however, I have to pose one question. Why do humans (especially women) change the way they talk when they turn to pets? Jill is an intelligent woman, and yet when she talks to me she says things like, "Mosey, are you a go-o-o-d dog? Yes you are! Yes you are! Moses is a very good boy!" And she says it with an overly sweet tone and makes funny faces as she talks. But it is not just Jill. Ladies at the YMCA or the grocery store come up to me and do the same sort of thing. What is that all about?

## Pets, Boredom and Cabin Fever
(March 5, 2010)

Are your pets "bored?" [Adjective, bored—feeling tired and irritable because of constantly being exposed to the uninteresting or because of having nothing interesting to do]

Our pets get bored and experience cabin fever just like we humans. If this boredom becomes intolerable your pet will get into trouble. The drapes might get torn, the stuffing in pillows might get scattered about, and the trash might be dragged throughout the house. Not a pretty picture. So what can we as pet owners do to help our pets fight off boredom and cabin fever?

Lots of people with fenced-in backyards assume that if they put the dog out in the yard he will find interesting things to do, but most dogs will simply find a spot and nap. If there are two or three dogs that get along and are in the yard together, they are more likely to play and amuse themselves, but a single dog in the backyard is too often lonely and bored. The same will be true if the single dog is left alone in the house for 8 or more hours every day while his owner is at work. Remember that dogs are social pack animals that need interactions with humans and/or other pets. Nevertheless, I am not suggesting that pet owners must run out and adopt a playmate for their dog. Further, I am not encouraging pet owners to stop working full-time, but there are some things pet owners can do to make life a little more interesting for the pooch.

Cesar Millan, National Geographic Channel's "The Dog Whisperer," makes the case that the most natural pastime for dogs is to walk in a pack. Walking the dog is good exercise for both you and your dog, but it is much more than just exercise. Taking the dog for a walk lets him smell new smells, see new sights, and bond with his owner as the pack leader. From a dog's point of view, a pack can be just one dog and one human. If you will be leaving your dog in the yard or in the house all day, it helps if you can walk the dog before you leave. The walk will tire him and a tired dog is a good dog!

You can also leave the radio on and prepare some "time consuming" toys with treats. I like to take two Kongs (rubber, practically non-destructible toys), smear the inside with a little peanut butter and fill each Kong with some kibble. I put these Kongs with kibble and peanut butter in the freezer the night before and present it to my dogs on my way out. My dogs are so excited about the Kong, they do not even notice I am leaving them. If you get the proper size kibbles, it can take the dog considerable time to lick the peanut butter clean and get the treats out of the center. When you feed the dog next, cut back on their food so the Kong treat does not put unwanted weight on your dog.

But dogs can also get bored even when you are home with them, especially when the weather is nasty outside and walks are difficult. When this happens, I have a few inside games I play with them. These are mental games that can sharpen their sense of smell and their memory skills. Moses' favorite is the shell game. To play the shell game you need three small opaque cups, a handful of kibble, and a slick low tabletop that the dog can reach with his nose. Start with one cup. Show your dog a piece of kibble and then place that kibble underneath the cup turned upside down. Encourage your dog to touch the cup with his nose. When he does, praise him and give him the treat. After a few repetitions, your dog will begin to realize that if he touches the cup with his nose, he will get the treat. At that point, add a second cup. Only one cup should have a treat under it, and to make the game fun, slide the cups around to see if you can trick your dog. If he noses the wrong cup, lift it up to show him it is empty, put it back down and let him try again. To teach your dog to use his nose to win this game, always place the treat under the same cup (put a small inconspicuous mark on one cup so you can tell which one it is), so that only one cup has the scent of the treat.

There are lots of other games you can play with your dog. Check out www.dogwise.com/index.cfm. You might also consult a book entitled *Fun and Games with Dogs* by Roy Hunter. Another book you might consult is *Hip Ideas for Hyper Dogs* by Amy Ammen and Kitty Foth-Regner.

What about cats? The key with cats is to get them involved with you interactively. A simple fishing pole with a feather tied to the line can give you and your cat lots of playtime together. By moving the pole and feather, you can get your cat to jump and turn. You might also tear off a piece of tin foil, roll it into a small tight ball and play hockey with your cat. The tin foil becomes the hockey puck. Use your imagination and through play you can help your pet stay mentally sharp, focused, and interested in their world.

### I Know I Am Not Supposed To Pet, But . . .
(March 12, 2010)

There is some confusion out there about when or if you can pet a service dog like Moses. Part of the confusion comes from the many different kinds of service dogs and the many different kinds of work they do. When Moses and I graduated from the Canine Companions for Independence Training Center, our professional trainers said that it was up to each of us as handlers to decide if we want people to interact with our dogs or not. They further emphasized that the rule for the general public is to always ask first before approaching any service dog or any type of unfamiliar dog, for that matter. The trainers also stressed that if you let your service dog interact with people, you must see to it that none of the admirers offer any treats to the dog. Finally they warned us about people who cannot resist rushing up to give the dog a "drive by" pat on the head or scratch under the chin.

Probably the best-known type of service dog is the "seeing eye dog." The public should never approach these working dogs because the dog's job can mean life or death for the blind handler. These guide dogs must stay focused at all times. Nevertheless, a service dog like Moses has less crucial jobs like companionship, picking up fallen out-of-reach objects and helping the handler with confidence in social situations. In other words, the stakes are not as high for a service dog like Moses. With that in mind, I frequently let people pet Moses even when he is on duty. In Mosey's case it is good practice to interact with strangers because he and I regularly visit the Wesley Health Care Center where his job is to engage the older patients and make them smile.

In sum, parents need to keep telling their children that a service dog is different from a pet and that they should always ask first before reaching out to pet any dog. I always appreciate parents that explain to their children that Moses is a trained helper dog that is allowed in a grocery store, restaurant, or shopping center. Older children might also be told that dogs like Moses are certified for public access and the Americans with Disabilities Act protects them from being denied access.

Turning now to another topic, I want to pat myself on the back because it is now one full year since I started writing my weekly pet column for *Saratoga Today*. To my amazement, after a year I have not yet run out of topics. I am still really enjoying the process of researching and writing about pets. It has also been fun to meet some of my readers around town. Just the other day I was in Hannaford and the woman in front of me in the check-out line exclaimed, "I know who you are!" I responded with, "Who am I?" She looked down at Moses and after a slight pause she said apologetically, "Well, I know he is Moses. But I guess I don't remember your name."

This was humbling since I was starting to think I was getting pretty famous locally with my pet columns. You see, for twenty-five years as a professor of anthropology at Skidmore College, I wrote a couple of books and many papers for academic journals, but practically no one (other than my husband Steve and my mom) ever read them. In contrast, with the *Saratoga Today* column people are actually reading what I write! Nonetheless, this nice woman in front of me at the Hannaford check-out counter only remembered Moses. So much for fame!!

―――――― 🐾 ――――――

## Animal Cruelty, Neglect and Abuse
(March 19, 2010)

There is no way to sugar coat the topics of animal cruelty, neglect, and abuse. It is sickening to hear about, to write about, or to read about any form of animal abuse. For pet lovers it is terribly hard to even comprehend. My husband Steve knows that when an animal cruelty story is coming up on the evening news, he needs to change the channel or hit the mute button because these violet crimes are so upsetting to me. So why then am I devoting my column this week to these horrific aspects of human/pet interaction? As much as I do not want to think about animals suffering at the hands of their owners or the hands of a bored neighborhood teenager, there have been so many cases of animal abuse in our area lately; I would be remiss to sweep it all under the rug. So without the gruesome details that the popular media seems to relish, I will write about the relationship between animal cruelty and other violet crimes that affect children, women, and the elderly. I will also write about Buster's law and recent efforts to strengthen this legislation.

The American Society for the Prevention of Cruelty to Animals (ASPCA) defines animal cruelty as "someone intentionally injuring or harming an animal or willfully depriving an animal of food, water or necessary medical care." Some signs of abuse or neglect include animals that cower in fear when approached by their owners, animals with untreated wounds on their body, animals with a limp, severely underweight animals, animals with patches of missing hair, animals with serious tick or flea infestations, or animals kept outside without shelter during extreme weather conditions. What is most interesting to me about animal abuse is that it is often found in families where child abuse, spousal abuse and/or elder abuse also occurs. In many cases animal abuse is the predictor of other violent crimes like rape or wife beating.

Sociologists, psychologists, and criminologists have shown a high correlation between childhoods with serious and repeated acts of animal cruelty, and adulthoods with other acts of violent crime committed against people. In one FBI study, imprisoned serial killers admitted killing or torturing pets when they were children. Further, some were themselves victims of child abuse. In other words, different kinds of abuse can foster still other types of abuse. The child who is abused may turn to torturing pets and as that child grows up he may commit violent crimes against people such as rape or murder.

These acts of cruelty and violence are interrelated and cyclical. They are all about control and power over another living creature. Children and pets are the most vulnerable abuse victims. Women are not far behind. The Humane Society of the United States (HSUS) found that in 85% of the homes where a woman is being abused, there is also an animal suffering from cruelty. Further, 71% of woman in a battered women's shelter reported their abuser either harmed a household pet or threatened to harm a pet, especially if the woman was emotionally attached to that pet.

The American Psychiatric Association lists animal cruelty as one of the behaviors that signal what they call "conduct disorder." Conduct disorder is a Psychiatric category marked by a pattern of repetitive behavior wherein the rights of others or social norms are violated. Clinical evidence suggests that animal cruelty usually marks the earliest stages of conduct disorder, sometimes as early as age seven or eight. Most professionals believe this is the time to intervene. Anthropologist Margaret Mead wrote,

"One of the most dangerous things that can happen to a child is to kill or torture an animal and get away with it."

Animal abuse is illegal in every state of the union. Some states see it as a misdemeanor while others, like New York, consider the worst cases as felony offences. Each state makes their own laws to protect animals from abuse, while the federal government has no role unless the abuse took place across state lines. In the state of New York we have Buster's law.

In 1999 Governor George Pataki signed Buster's Law, named for a tabby cat that was cruelly killed by his 16-year-old owner (currently in prison for rape). Assemblyman Jim Tedisco the original sponsor of the bill, has recently advocated for ways to strengthen Buster's Law. Tedisco wants the maximum fine of $5,000 to be raised to $10,000 and the possible prison terms to be raised from 2 years to 4 years. Tedisco also advocates horses be included as protected companion animals. The bill to strengthen Buster's Law (A8444) is currently stuck in the Agriculture Committee. Concerned citizens who want A8444 to pass can send letters to William Magee, chair of the Agriculture Committee. Magee's Albany office address is LOB 828, Albany, New York 12248.

## Suspecting and Reporting Animal Abuse in Your Community
(March 26, 2010)

As a follow-up to last week's column on Buster's Law and the relationship between animal abuse and other types of violent domestic crimes, today I focus on what to do if you suspect animal abuse. Who should you contact? Will you be taken seriously? What agencies might become involved in an animal abuse case? What should you do if no action is taken to protect the animal(s) in question?

According to the American Society for the Prevention of Cruelty to Animals (ASPCA), "Animal cruelty occurs when someone intentionally injures or harms an animal or when a person willfully deprives an animal of food, water or necessary medical care." In other words, neglect can be a form of cruelty and abuse. Animals cannot speak up for themselves when they are in a situation of neglect or abuse. Nevertheless, good people who are perceptive can and do report animal abuse. In doing so, these good people may have prevented further suffering for a frightened cat or an emotionally "shut down dog."

If your community has a police department, contacting them is the first step. If your community does not have a police department, try the Sheriff's Office and/or the New York State Police. In either case, provide the authorities with a concise and clearly written statement describing what you witnessed as an indication of abuse. Photographs of abuse are useful, but do not take unnessasary risks to get a photograph. While such a report may be given anonymously, a busy town or state police department, as well as a busy Sheriff's Office will probably take you more seriously if you sign your name to the report. They will also take you more seriously if you follow-up on your complaint.

If you do not get satisfactory action from your local police department, the New York State Police, or the Sheriff's Office, you still have some other options. You can contact the SPCA of Upstate New York, located in Queensbury, New York. Their phone number is (518) 798-3500. You can also contact your local Animal Control Officers for advice.

If you need to report animal cruelty at a racetrack, you must contact the New York Racing Association (NYRA). If you see animal abuse at a pet store, you need to contact the U.S. Department of Agriculture (USDA). Likewise, if you see animals treated poorly by a breeder, it is the USDA that can hear your complaint. Along with keeping notes on the abuse, it will help if you also keep track of to whom you spoke and when. This may be very helpful when you need to follow up on your report of abuse.

Sometimes veterinarians who suspect abuse will report their concerns to the appropriate authorities. There are eleven states that actually mandate that they do so. The American Animal Hospital Association's (AAHA) position on vets reporting abuse states, "Since veterinarians have a responsibility to the welfare of animals and the public and can be the first to detect animal abuse in a family, they should take an active role in detecting, preventing and reporting animal abuse. Nevertheless, reporting should only be required when client education has failed or in situations in which immediate intervention is indicated and only when the law exempts veterinarians from civil and criminal liability for reporting."

Before closing, I want to make people aware of one type of neglect that too often begins with good intentions but tragically can end in disease or even death for animals. Frequently referred to as "hoarding," this type of abuse is the accumulation of large numbers of animals that because of their numbers are living in extremely unsanitary conditions. Sadly with these overcrowded conditions disease can spread quickly and become deadly for the animals and even for their human keepers.

Let me urge parents and teachers everywhere to take the time to teach children about kindness to animals. This lesson of kindness is important in their interactions with pets as well as their interactions with siblings, friends and neighbors. The simple truth is children who display cruelty towards animals are more likely to be cruel to the people in their social world.

## The Black Magic Cat
(April 1, 2010)

At different times over this past year, Jill let Vida, Moses, and even Sully (the cat) take over her Whiskers and Tales column. This week she finally agreed to let me have a turn. I am Magic, the newest member of our pack. Jill adopted me last October during the annual Meow Luau, hosted by Friends of the Saratoga County Animal Shelter. The Meow Luau is a fall event featuring adult cats in need of homes. You see, adult cats like me are passed over all the time for kittens. Sure kittens are cute, but they grow into adult cats in no time. They also lack the grace, style, beauty, and wisdom of a more mature creature like me!

I know Jill has been writing lately about animal abuse and neglect. Being a black cat, I know something about mistreatment. You see, black cats are often treated badly because we are associated with the occult, bad luck, and even evil witches. This is all silly superstition, but the legacy stands and black cats like me suffer because of it. As a kitten, I remember being taunted by some mean kids and somehow I ended up in the county shelter. Next a very kind woman from H.O.P.E. (Homes For Orphaned Pets Exist) took me out of the shelter. The people at H.O.P.E. found me a foster home. At first I thought this was to be my forever home, but no. I lived in three different foster homes before I finally landed in my forever home with Jill, Steve, Vida, Moses, and Sully.

My best human friend is Steve. I sleep perched on his stomach every night. If he turns to his side, I just move to perch myself on his hip rather than his stomach. Steve often calls me Mek-Mek because he says I am a talker and one of the sounds I make is "Mek-Mek" which means, "Pay attention to me." At first I didn't play much, but now that I am finally feeling secure and loved, I am playing with crumpled pipe cleaners that bounce when I give them a swat. I am also playing with Sully, although I would say our relationship is one of love/hate. We swat each other, pounce on each other, chase each other and hiss, but we also sleep by each other peacefully.

My message to our readers during this time of year when so many kittens are born is please do not be fooled by cute. Consider adopting an adult cat, and spay or neuter your kittens and cats to curb the problem of too many homeless felines. In addition, I want to tell you all about an event coming up that is fun and supports H.O.P.E. so they can continue their important animal rescue work. The event is the annual Walk for the Animals.

Participants in the walk will meet in Congress Park near the pavilion closest to Broadway. There will be refreshments, gifts, photographs, and registration. All walkers will come with pledges from their neighbors, family, and friends. The walkers who raise the most pledge money will win special prizes. The participants will then parade up Broadway to Skidmore and back. Most will have a dog with them, but if you do not have a dog, you can still walk. Frankly, I can do without the canines, but lots of people adore their dogs, even though cats rule and dogs drool. Nevertheless, the walk promises to be fun and of great benefit for many orphaned pets like me before I found my forever home with help from H.O.P.E. and Friends of the Saratoga County Animal Shelter. By the way, I hear the new shelter is coming along and looking good. Check it out!

## An Extraordinary Book About An Extraordinary Dog
(April 9, 2010)

I often pass over books about dogs because so many of them are simply stories with heartbreaking plots. Ever since I saw Old Yeller as a kid with no warning about the ending, I have been leery of dog stories. So when someone told me I really should read *Merle's Door: Lessons from a Freethinking Dog*, I put it on my shelf and there it sat until I was desperately looking for something to read and all I could find was this dog book by Ted Kerasote. After reading the first few pages, I was hooked. It turned out to be such a wonderful read – one that made me laugh, cry, and rethink some of my assumptions about dogs in general, and about my two dogs (Vida and Moses), in particular.

*Merle's Door* takes place in the deserts, mountains, and villages of Utah and Montana. It is a true story about how the author lived as a single middle-aged man who, when he was not writing, was hiking, skiing, and hunting in these Western states. On one of his excursions into the Utah deserts, he came across a lost or abandoned young adult dog that was thin, but appeared to be surviving in the wilderness on his own. Ted had been looking to adopt a purebred puppy, but this "free ranging" dog became irresistible especially when he seemed to have picked Ted to be his human. Ted writes the dog looked into his eyes and said, "you need a dog and I am it."

Ted and Merle's relationship was one of partners, rather than human as indisputable leader and dog as follower. Kerasote's approach to dogs is the exact opposite of Cesar Millan's approach (the Dog Whisperer). Millan argues that dogs need and want the human to be their pack leader. On the other hand, Kerasote argues that dogs need freedom to reach their potential. They need to come and go as they wish—hence, the symbolic and practicable importance of

Ted making Merle a dog door at their cabin. Ted did not like to put Merle in a collar or on a leash. He did everything he could to respect Merle as his equal.

Kerasote's views can work in areas with low population density, but for those of us who live in the cities or suburbs, having a dog running free is not only illegal, it is dangerous. Nevertheless, only 50 years ago, Saratoga Springs was small enough that there were dogs without leash and collar that would roam Broadway and like Merle, these dogs would make the rounds to all the dog-friendly stores and offices.

There are aspects of Kerasote's approach that can be adopted even in densely populated areas. For example, Kerasote is a keen observer of his dog's body language. After reading the book I found that I became more in tune with Vida and Mosey's body language. This is key to developing communication between human and dog. Kerasote writes, "Dog owners who hold 'conversations' with their dogs will know exactly what I mean. Those who don't—as well as those who find the whole notion of conversing with a dog absurd—may want to consider that humans have shared a longer and more intimate partnership with dogs than with any other domestic animal, starting before civilization existed."

The above quote is also an example of the way the author weaves together the story of Merle along with anthropological, psychological, and behavioral scientific studies that support his ideas that dogs can be emotional, sensitive, and intelligent animals that can feel love, disappointment, jealousy, and other emotions typically reserved for humans. By observing Merle's body language the author "translates" what he believes the dog is communicating.

While this translation is often delightful, the reader needs to remember this is only Kerasote's interpretation. Further, most of these interpretations are examples of anthropomorphism or projecting human characteristics and behaviors on to nonhuman animals. The author defends himself by putting his observations into the context of the human need to make sense of other people or animals. He writes, "There'd be no human intercourse, or it would be enormously impoverished, without our attempting to use our emotions as templates—as starting points—to map the feelings of other people or species."

This book raises questions about how dogs think. It also addresses the nurture/nurture debate, what separates humans from other animals, and the practice of euthanasia. This dog book is much more than a story of heartbreak, although you may need some tissues at the end. *Merle's Door* is an enjoyable and informative book about love, freedom, and the life of a very special dog named Merle. Give yourself a treat and get a copy from the library or the bookstore. I promise it is a book you will not soon forget.

## Disruption In the Pack
(April 30, 2010)

Regular readers of this column know our household includes two humans (Steve and me), two dogs (Vida and Moses), and two cats (Sully and Magic). My husband, Steve calls the two dogs and the two cats "The Critters," and I like to refer to the six of us as "The Pack." Just after Easter this year, Steve and all the critters as well as myself experienced disruption in our little pack. We all were clearly affected by this, but each had his or her way of reacting to the disorder in our little pack. It all began with Steve feeling poorly.

Steve, like so many men who would rather die than admit to needing a doctor, a medical procedure, or hospitalization tried to keep quiet about how ill he really felt. After several days, he could no longer hide his condition. I knew something was terribly wrong and so did the critters. By the time he finally agreed to go to the hospital, he was too weak to get into my car so I could drive him there. Instead I had to call 911 and an ambulance arrived. The critters watched with wide eyes as he was carried out on a stretcher.

After the ambulance left with Steve, I began to cry at our kitchen table. The critters watched me from a distance. Finally I felt Moses' chin on my lap. I gave him a squeeze and dried my tears. Then I called the hospital and I learned that Steve was going into emergency surgery. Following surgery, Steve was in the intensive care unit where he would be for the next three weeks! I will not bore my readers with all the details of Steve's medical condition, except to say it was a very stressful time for all of us.

When the cats realized Steve was not going to be right back, they began to act differently. Sully and Magic started to "hunt" in our basement. I had never seen a mouse in our house, but Sully and Magic proved me wrong. They appeared to be playing together, but on closer inspection, they were batting around a frightened little field mouse. They chased it into my room. After a few minutes they came out without the mouse. They both looked dejected. Apparently the mouse found a hole in the floorboards and vanished into the basement. Later that evening, I opened the door that joins our kitchen to the garage and basement. There sat a very still little mouse. It was dead. Was it an offering for me in my time of need? Sully strutted by me as I stared down at the little mouse. I thanked Sully for his offering.

Magic also displayed some new behaviors. She has always been Steve's cat. She would follow him around the house and sleep curled up next to him. Now that Steve was gone she began to seek affection from me. Usually she ignored me because Steve was her man. Now with him gone, she settled for me to give her some loving. Magic also began leaving little piles of partially digested and regurgitated Purina I cat food—on the sink, on my computer, and on my bedside table.

When I went in to see Steve in the ICU, Moses, my service dog that goes everywhere with me, sniffed at Steve's hand and backed away. He had trouble settling down. He knew something was wrong. Over the next days and weeks he went with me to see Steve many times, but until Steve could talk to him and give him a reassuring pat on the head, Moses could not relax in the ICU.

Twelve-year-old Vida's response to all the drama surrounding Steve's emergency was to sleep. She did not want to go out, refused to eat and seemed to temporarily shut down. A couple of friends who have their own dogs offered to take Vida for a few days while things calmed down. This helped me, but for Moses this was just one more disruption. Where was Vida? When I called my fiend about bringing her back, Moses must have heard me say her name several times during the conversation, because he jumped up and began looking for her in all the rooms of our house. When my friend brought her back later that day, Moses was clearly excited to see her and that she was back where she belonged.

What all this showed me is that our dogs and cats are sensitive and emotional creatures. This revelation may seem obvious to most pet lovers, but until I saw how Sully, Magic, Vida and Moses reacted after Steve went into the hospital, I did not really appreciate how emotional our pets are when their routines are disrupted and a member of the pack is missing.

## Reuniting the Pack and Other Matters
(May 7, 2010)

Steve came home from the hospital at last. I expected the cats to rejoice at his return, but to my surprise both cats ignored him. Magic did not even come out to greet him. Sully came out to see Steve but then went on his way. Were they punishing him for being gone so long? After about 12 hours, they came around some, but they still were acting aloof. Since Moses had seen Steve every day in the hospital, I was not surprised that he did not make a fuss over his return. Vida did not take too much notice of Steve's return either, but with her doggy dementia, who knows how much she understands anyway? So without much fanfare our pack was reunited.

Turning now to other pet news, I want to let everyone know that spring is kitten season and the Saratoga County Animal Shelter is overflowing with many litters of kittens. There are homeless kittens everywhere in the shelter as well as many homeless mother cats. If you have been thinking about adopting a kitten or an adult cat, now may be the time to bring one home. You will find every color, every hair length, and every disposition among all those cats at the shelter. Perhaps you can open your heart and give a feline a chance.

Why are there so many homeless kittens and cats? In large part it is because owners do not always spay or neuter their cats. Remember that an altered cat makes a better pet. They stay closer to home and are less likely to fight and get injured. They also are less likely to stain your furniture or carpeting. Furthermore, if the cost of spaying or neutering is a problem, contact one or more of the following:

Friends of Animals (800) 321-7387

Cat Care Coalition (518) 466-8484

Guilderhaven, Love me Spay me Program (518) 861-6861

H.O.P.E. (518) 248-8484

Columbia Greene Humane Society (518) 828-6861

Montgomery County SPCA (518) 842-8050

Quaintance House Animal Protection League (518) 692-9848

Robins Nest Cat Rescue (518) 868-9930

Another reason for cat overpopulation is that many owners want their female cat to have at least one litter before she is spayed. They reason that the children in the family will benefit from seeing a birth and the creation of new life. This is fine, but at what cost? Perhaps the more important lesson is that the over population of cats can tragically end in euthanasia because there simply are not enough homes for all the felines in our communities.

In closing, I want to mention that Moses and I are flying out to Southern California this week. I have flown with Vida before, but this will be the first time with Mr. Moses. We will be in transit for about seven hours. I hope he does as well riding in the cabin with me as did Vida years ago. When we return I will let you know how it went. By the way, Moses passed his six-month test back at the CCI training center on Long Island. It was fun to see again all the students and dogs from our graduating class. The test was administered in a shopping mall. We had to show how we manage overly affectionate strangers, loud noises, excited kids, elevators, and automatic doors. They even had to stay in a down position while the instructors dropped kibble all around them. Moses did not move a muscle even when a kibble landed about three inches from his nose. Now that we passed, we do not have another test for a year. After that it will be every three years.

---

## Mosey's First Ride on an Airplane
(May 14, 2010)

Remember me? I'm Moses, Jill's faithful, smart and oh-so handsome service dog. A couple of days ago Jill and I flew to southern California for her mother's memorial. The flight was really long and I had to wait for ten hours before I could find a patch of green to relieve myself! I learned that airports are short on grass and long on pavement. Nevertheless, I made it and Jill was very proud of me.

When the plane took off I was a little afraid but soon I relaxed. We sat in the first row of seats behind first class. I sat or stretched out on the floor in front of Jill. There also was a nice lady that sat by Jill. This lady made a fuss over me, as did all the flight attendants. They offered me water, but I refused because I knew it would be a long time before I could "go." Everyone wanted to give me cookies but Jill said no to that because I was working. Sometimes it is hard, however, to be a good boy and not beg for a cookie when Jill is not looking.

During the long flight the lady sitting next to us seemed to be going into a dangerous state. Most humans do not pick up on the subtle signs of danger that I felt sitting next to this woman. Smart dogs like me notice these things. I started getting restless. I pawed at the lady in an effort to warn her of the danger. Jill apologized for my change in behavior. She said to the lady, "I don't know why he is acting like this." Then she said, "Moses leave the nice lady alone."

I kept it up because I needed to warn the lady before something terrible happened. Suddenly she caught on. She was diabetic and she was about to go into what they call "diabetic shock." As soon as she realized what was happening she asked for some orange juice. After she drank it all down, the signs of danger left. She was going to be all right. Good thing dogs know these things, because humans so often miss the signs.

Some canines are so good at reading signs of danger they can warn people of seizures or a loss of consciousness before these things happen. Some of us can warn humans of fire or earthquakes. These things can be deadly for people so it is important they listen to perceptive canines when they try to warn them. It is our gift to humans, but the humans must be receptive or our warning goes unheeded.

This is a true story. If you don't believe me just ask Jill! Next time Jill will write about California and my first time swimming in the Pacific Ocean. It was really fun and it helped to cheer Jill up even though she was sad about her mother.

## Swimming Dogs
(May 21, 2010)

California was wonderful—perfect weather, no earthquakes, and happy reunions with family and old friends. I grew up in Laguna Beach, California and attended Laguna Beach High School, class of '68 (I am dating myself). Looking the town over now, I realized when I was a kid I did not fully appreciate how beautiful Laguna was. Views of the Pacific Ocean are breathtaking and the flowers everywhere are colorful and fragrant. The town has changed some, but it is still a paradise. Moses and I had a terrific time. The highlight for him was swimming in the ocean.

This was Moses' first time on the beach. He retrieved sticks and Frisbees until we were all ready to drop. We kept him on a long leash, which was a good thing because at one point he was swimming way out to sea and not looking back. He looked like a seal in the water. He even rode a few waves to bring himself to shore. I watched from the cliffs as my niece, my brother, and my sister-in-law kept him busy playing and then washing him off in an open shower when we were ready to leave.

Watching Moses swim in the ocean made me wonder about swimming dogs. Are all dogs hard-wired to know how to swim? Do some dog breeds make better swimmers than others? Are there any dangers associated with dog aquatics? Are there sports events featuring dog swimmers? Are there dog friendly vacation spots where one can bring their dog along and let him swim in a lake, stream, or pool?

The best dogs for swimming include all the retrievers (Labradors, Goldens, Chesapeake Bays), water spaniels, setters, poodles, barbets (French water dogs), Kerry blue terriers, Hungarian pulis, and Portuguese water dogs (Obama's dog). Some of these dogs actually have webbed feet and waterproof coats that dry off quickly. Dogs that are not great swimmers include Basset Hounds, Bulldogs, Dachshunds, Pugs, Corgis, as well as Scottish and Boston terriers. Relatively heavy bodies and short legs make swimming difficult for these breeds. Greyhounds are not strong swimmers either. Dogs in the first group typically love the water and in the latter group the dogs are often afraid of the water.

As a matter of safety, owners should never leave their dogs unattended at pools, lakes, or the ocean. Even if they are strong swimmers, dogs can get into trouble and should be supervised near water. Up here in the Northeast, we have all heard stories of dogs venturing out on the spring ice only to fall through and become in desperate need of help. Dogs can also tire in ocean currents or in fast moving rivers.

Dogs that do not take to the water naturally can be taught to swim. This should be attempted only when the dog is calm and focused. They should never be tossed into the water without preparation. Dogs should be encouraged with toys and treats to enter the water. If the "dog paddle" does not come naturally, the owner can support the dog's midsection and hindquarters in the water until he starts paddling on his own. It is also important to show the dog how to get out of the water.

In terms of sporting events that feature dogs in the water, DockDogs, Big Air, and Extreme Vertical are all events of growing popularity. They began as a grass roots movement in 2000 and now are regularly featured on ESPN, ABC, and CBS sports. The dogs run off a dock and land in the water. The height and the length of the jump are measured. Anyone with a dog and a throw toy can participate. It looks like terrific fun. DogDock clubs are being organized all over the country. For more information on DockDogs, visit www.dockdogs.com or pick up a copy of Dockdogs Magazine.

Vacations for you and your dog are popular in many parts of the country. Lists of dog-friendly hotels, rentals, and vacations can be found on the Internet. One example is Happy Tails Resort and Spa in Auburn or Enumclaw, both in Washington state. Happy Tails features the Ultimate Dog Pool. They are located on a two-acre, eight-foot-high fenced area on a 20-acre family farm. Sounds pretty nice, doesn't it?

## Springtime, Finally!
(May 27, 2010)

It's Moses here. You know, Moses II, Jill's devoted, trustworthy, smart, and handsome (if I may say so myself) service dog from Canine Companions for Independence. Jill has been really busy working on her book lately (she says she has been inspired and when inspiration hits a writer must act), so she asked me to do her Whiskers and Tales column this time. Jill's cat Sully also wants to say something. Sully just wants to brag that he caught his first mouse last night and ceremoniously presented it to Jill and her dinner party guests!

The first thing I want to tell you about is my participation in the 8th Annual Walk for the Animals last month. It is a fundraiser for H.O.P.E., which stands for Homes for Orphaned Pets Exist. The nice people from H.O.P.E. find homeless dogs and cats forever homes. Because there are too many homeless dogs and cats they are opening a low-cost Spay and Neuter clinic. This clinic is opening on June 1 at 4255 Rt. 50, Wilton. The clinic is very important because getting your dogs and cats spayed or neutered is the only way we can reduce the homeless pet problem. Clients must qualify and make an appointment. At first the clinic will be open only one day a week. For more information call (518) 248-0358.

So anyway, the dog walk was lots of fun. It had a Mardi Gras theme. Some of the humans put on masks, beads, hats, and other silly stuff. They even put costumes on some of the dogs! Humiliation! Jill spared me from wearing a costume, but she did put a purple H.O.P.E. t-shirt on me. There were all kinds of dogs: big ones, little ones, mutts, and pure breds. Everyone got along. We walked behind a big red fire engine and some belly dancers. There were prizes for the best dressed dog, the best tail wagger, and the dog with the best smile. I won the prize for the best smile. It was a box of dog treats.

I also want to remind those of you who are gardeners that spring planting can pose some dangers for pets. Many plants, if ingested can cause liver failure in cats and dogs. These include sago palm and other Cycads—even mushrooms. In addition, rhododendron, azalea, lily of the valley, oleander, rosebay, and foxglove can damage your pet's heart if consumed. Further, ingesting fertilizer can upset your pet's digestive tract—yukk!

If you have a compost pile, be sure it is fenced off so dogs cannot get into the moldy food that can be toxic. In addition, pesticides need to be stored properly and always follow directions concerning exposure to pets. If you spread mulch, keep an eye on your pets and see that they do not consume any, especially cocoa mulch.

Another hazard may be garden tools that are not kept in a safe place; particularly hazardous are tools that are sharp, dirty and rusty. Remember as well pets can develop allergies to food, plants, dust or pollen. If you suspect allergies consult your veterinarian.

In closing, I want to recommend a good book about a Canine Companion for Independence dog like me. The book is by Dean Koontz, entitled *A Big Little Life*. It is about a girl dog named Trixie who happens to be a cousin of mine. This really nice lady we met at the dog walk gave the book to Jill just because she is a good person who loves dogs and people who also love dogs!

Enjoy spring and keep your pets safe.

## Pets as Antidepressants and Pets as Obsessions
(May 28, 2010)

Dogs, cats, birds, hamsters, and even reptiles can help people overcome a mild or moderate depression. Unlike Prozac or Zoloft, however, there are not so many nasty side effects from simply caring for a pet. Positive interaction with pets can even reduce the risk of the more serious, clinical depressions. In short, feelings of sorrow, dread, loneliness, hopelessness, and meaninglessness can be reduced when a pet enters the picture. Pets may not cure a depression, but they can make them more manageable, less frequent and shorter in duration.

There have been academic studies supporting the notion that pet ownership has mental and psychosocial benefits for humans. These benefits include exercise, affection, leadership, companionship, and routine. These five benefits are all the result of being a responsible pet owner. For example, how can I be depressed staring out the window when our cats Sully and Magic wind in and out of my ankles crying that it is time for me to feed them? How can I ignore our dog Moses when he brings me the ball, drops it at my feet, and dances around eager for our after dinner game of catch? How can I stay in bed with the covers over my head when our other dog, Vida brings a leash to me in hopes of our morning walk? Pets do not take days off. They need our care every day!

Taking the dogs out for a walk is good for the dogs and the human. Fresh air and exercise are known as depression fighters with both physical and psychological rewards. In addition, stroking and holding a cat reduces anxiety and can even lower blood pressure. Perhaps these positive processes explain why many nursing home residents (frequently depressed about their loss of independence) respond so positively when I bring Moses around to visit. Hopefully, as more and more hospital and nursing home administrators realize there is power in visits from pets, more programs for regular pet visitations will be established.

More then six million older people suffer from clinical depression. At the same time animal shelters are overflowing with dogs and cats that need forever homes. If we could just get the animals and the depressed folks together, the world would be a better place for humans and domesticated animals.

Turning now to another situation—a much sadder one for the animals—we see how pets can also become the obsession of individuals. These are people who cannot help themselves from bringing home more pets than they can feed or shelter. Hoarding is an example of obsessive-compulsive disorder and has been a topic of much interest in the media lately. There are people who hoard all kinds of material goods and do so to the point of completely filling up their home, garage, and basement. Animal hoarding is just one particular type of hoarding.

An animal hoarder is someone who may start with good intentions, but the expense, work, and responsibility of caring for the animals they obsess over become too much for them. Typically animal hoarders are in denial about their hoarding. They do not see the malnutrition, the overcrowding, or the dying animals in their home. Unfortunately, even after the ASPCA takes action and removes the neglected animals, the perpetrators simply go back to hoarding animals again. Without long-term psychological intervention and in some cases jail time, there are only short-term solutions to the problem.

Nearly 250,000 animals are victims of animal hoarding each year. Unlike other animal abusers, hoarders do not accept or recognize the cruelty they impose on the animals that do not get even minimal care. Officers who investigate animal hoarding often find feces and urine on the furniture, floors, and countertops. In some of the worst cases, decaying animal carcasses are found alongside living animals.

In closing, if you suffer from depression, you might consider a pet to give you unconditional love. Remember having a pet can take your focus off your problems and turn your thoughts toward caring for that pet. As an antidepressant, a pet can do you considerable good. On the other hand, if you suspect an obsession with animals that results in animal hoarding in your neighborhood, you need to contact your local police department or the ASPCA. Stand up for the animals!

## What It Takes To Make a Service Dog
(June 4, 2010)

People often come up to Moses and me saying, "What a calm dog. I wish my dog would act like that!" What rushes through my mind when I hear these comments, is what it actually does take to make a dog like Moses. To begin it takes selective breeding. Only dogs with good health, intelligence, confidence, and a calm demeanor will become breeders of the next generation. Further, it takes a devoted puppy raiser and an understanding public. Then it takes a period of professional training and proper placement with a disabled individual. This process typically takes about two years. Finally, it takes regular training throughout the dog's career to keep him mentally and physically sharp. Today I want to focus on the devoted puppy raiser and the need for an understanding public. I recently read that a local man was not pleased when one of those puppy raisers brought her young trainee to the pool at the Saratoga YMCA.

Moses and I go the YMCA regularly for my morning swim. Moses stays on the side of the pool as I do my laps. I know he loves to swim, but I also know that he will not jump in the pool after me. Instead he resists his urge to swim because I tell him, "Moses down, Moses wait." When I finish my laps and am lifted out of the pool on a wonderful piece of equipment donated to the Saratoga YMCA, Moses follows me out of the pool area and into the women's shower room. While I shower he waits under the counter where swimmers dry their hair. Once I am dressed (with help from Donna, a very kind employee of the Saratoga YMCA) and I am ready to go, Moses calmly follows me out of the building to start our day together.

On two occasions, Barbara, a friend of mine who is a puppy raiser for Guiding Eyes for the Blind, brought her young retriever, Lorna to the pool while she participated in a swim class. Lorna did very well, but she occasionally let out a bark. It was not constant barking, but simply a few barks letting Barbara know she would rather be in the pool with her and the other swimmers. Nevertheless, Lorna held her ground and waited at the side of the pool.

Part of a puppy raiser's job is to expose the puppies to all kinds situations so when she graduates with her new human partner, she will remain calm and confident in any setting. Most people understand this, and the YMCA with all the excited children and lots of action is a perfect place to teach Lorna to remain calm and confident. Other places Barbara has taken Lorna include restaurants, the mall, and the grocery store. In addition, Barbara gets advice from her regional representative of Guiding Eyes for the Blind. This advice comes in classes and discussions. For all this, Barbara gets no monetary compensation. She gives her time and covers the costs of feeding and caring for the puppy because she knows her puppy will one day change someone's life for the better.

I guess it takes a village to raise a service dog. The training continues throughout the working life of the dog. Once the dog is retired, he will be replaced with another. Sometimes the disabled handler will request that the retired dog stay on as a pet. When my first service dog, Vida, reached twelve-years-old I retired her, but wanted to keep her with me as a pet. Early on when I first began writing this column, my readers heard all about Vida. I still have a few people from those early days ask me about Vida. I assure them that despite her whitening muzzle, Vida is healthy and enjoys going with Moses and me for our shorter afternoon walks.

The message here is a thank you to all the establishments like the YMCA that permit a puppy raiser like Barbara to train her charge in a busy public place. The dogs grow up to be calm, affectionate, and attentive like Vida and Moses; they grow up to be valuable helpers for the disabled. I have always felt that my service dogs are the best part (maybe the only good part) of being disabled. Service dogs are the silver lining in the often frustrating and sometimes distressing world of the disabled. Furthermore, none of this would happen without the devotion and care of the puppy raiser as well as an understanding public.

## Holistic Veterinarian Medicine
(June 18, 2010)

Last week I mentioned that we now have a new veterinarian in town that practices holistic medicine for animals. I admitted that I knew very little about this form of medicine for animals. Once I could ignore the little voice in my head that said, "This stuff is too folksy and strange," I could admit that I really was interested to learn more about it. The following is some of what I learned:

Holistic vet medicine is made up of healing techniques and an underlying philosophical approach to healing. The techniques might involve administering herbs to the animal and the underlying philosophy is based on the idea that all creatures of the earth are interrelated and need to be approached as part of an integrated whole. Does that sound too mysterious, too weird, or too mystical? Let me try again with a concrete example.

A dog is brought into the vet's office with a limp. For a holistic vet it is not enough to simply look at the dog's leg or foot, but rather to look at that leg or foot in relation to the other parts of his body as well as considering how they function within the dog's physical, social, and natural worlds. Still sound too esoteric? Let me try once again.

A holistic examination begins with a complete look at the animal, taking into consideration his whole body, social environment, natural environment, daily activities, diet, and his relationship with his owner. All these things can and often do impact on the health of the animal. Therefore if the animal is ill, all these factors must be considered before any treatment can be recommended and administered. Does this still sound mysterious? Let me turn to a definition offered by Wikipedia, the free encyclopedia.

According to Wikipedia, "Holistic veterinary medicine is a type of veterinary medicine that uses alternative medicine in the treatment of animals. The philosophy of a holistic veterinarian emphasizes empathy and minimal invasiveness. Alternative therapies offered by a holistic veterinarian may include, but are not limited to, acupuncture, herbal remedies, homeopathy, and chiropractic. OK, that is clearer, but what is homeopathy?

Homeopathy is based on the turn of the 18th century idea that "like cures like." Any substance that can produce symptoms in a healthy animal can cure similar symptoms in a sick animal. For example an onion is a substance that might make your dog's eyes to water and burn. If your dog has an attack of hay fever with watery eyes and burning nose, a homeopathic remedy made from an onion should relieve his symptoms.

Of course holistic veterinary medicine in general, and homeopathic treatments specifically, are controversial. Medical science wants proof and use of the scientific method. Nevertheless, holistic medicine for humans and pets is defended and used by people and their pets in many areas of our country. If some of it makes sense and the standard medical model is not giving your pet relief, you might try a holistic practitioner. Some people prefer to start with a holistic approach and if that is not helping, turn to standard medical help.

After looking over my draft for this column on holistic medicine for pets, my husband (and my at-home editor), reminded me that years ago when our beloved German Shepherd Nick lost control over his hind legs, we turned to acupuncture. We had tried everything else and felt that we had nothing to lose. It did not help him, but it gave us some piece of mind that we had tried everything we could think of to try. Nick was a beautiful and very sweet shepherd but we finally agreed that to keep him going was actually a selfish need in us and not in his best interest. We said good-bye to Nick after ten wonderful years with him.

## The Joy of Adopting an Older Cat
(July 2, 2010)

It makes me so sad when I learn that after four, eight, ten years or more, the owner of a cat surrenders her to the shelter. The reason given on the form the owner must fill out may be "family allergies," "moving to a place where cats are not allowed," "can no longer afford to care for the animal" or "doesn't get along with young children, a new puppy or a new kitten." I am sure sometimes the reasons given are true, but I can't help wonder if some owners just lose interest in caring for their cat. I wonder if in our throw-away society some owners rationalize, "Hell, its just a cat anyway."

I also wonder how much time and effort went into ensuring that young children, new puppies or new kittens are taught to respect and get along with the older cat. Sometimes it just takes a little patience and time to bring harmony back to the family. Making the effort to keep the older cat is a positive lesson for the children in the family. Children need to learn that pets are not disposable, but rather a long-term commitment and a responsibility. Further, they are living creatures that feel pain, loss, and in many cases, feel an attachment to humans.

Surrendered or stray adult cats are at a terrible disadvantage in a shelter situation because people are so attracted to the amusing antics of kittens. They pass over many adorable and sweet natured older cats and turn instead to the kittens. The cats available for adoption at the SCAS one week included Angel (8 year-old spayed female), Bernie (9 year-old neutered male), Jack (10 year-old neutered male), Maxwell (4 year-old neutered male), Rita (6 year-old), and Lucky (older adult neutered male).

Our cat Magic taught us the joys of adopting an older cat. At first when we brought her home she was shy and frightened. She had been in three different foster homes in less than a year. She was afraid to trust humans after being abandoned by them. Unfortunately, as a black cat she also suffered from superstitions and an association with evil, bad luck, and the occult. This association, consciously or unconsciously, may have made it easier to abandon Magic. In short, life was not kind to this beautiful black cat with large expressive blue/green eyes.

My husband was the first to get past Magic's insecurities. Soon she began sleeping by him but during the day she would hide in the bedroom under the bed, in the closet or behind the headboard. Sometimes she hid herself so well we began to worry that she got out of the house somehow. Luckily this was not the case.

For six months Magic ignored me, but when Steve went into the hospital for three weeks last March, Magic began to turn to me for a scratch behind her ears or a pat on the head. When Steve returned home, Magic ignored him. After a couple of weeks, however, she forgave him his absence and started sleeping by him again. Nonetheless, her new relationship with me continued. At this point Magic also developed her love/hate relationship with our other cat, Sully.

Magic and Sully spar with each other. Magic, who may have learned to swat other cats in the streets, always wins in a playful sparing match with Sully. For each slap that Sully gives Magic, she comes back with two quicker ones that land on Sully. She is that fast and Sully backs off looking a bit dejected.

The exciting thing about Magic is that every day she is more confident, more willing to be held, and she is even becoming affectionate. Magic is coming out of her shell and it is gratifying to see. I even find her sleeping peacefully in the sun on my bed each afternoon. The dogs, Vida and Moses leave her alone and she ignores them as well. Yes, there is peace in our home of two cats, two dogs, and two humans.

Next time you are looking for a new feline companion, think of Magic and all the adult cats that need forever homes. Just think, you could help restore trust of humans even in a cat with a history of abandonment.

## Year of the Fish and the Age of Aquariums
(July 9, 2010)

Most of my columns focus on dogs or cats. I also have written about hamsters, parakeets, and rabbits, but usually it is dogs and/or cats. For families with allergies, dogs, cats, rabbits, hamsters, and even parakeets are probably out of the question. The same goes for families with landlords that do not permit pets. So what can these families do? Some may turn to fish. Fish can be colorful, amusing to watch, and they can be very calming. I guess that is why so many doctors' offices have fish aquariums in the waiting rooms. Watching colorful fish gracefully meandering through gently moving plants or miniature castles give the waiting patient something to think about besides feeling poorly or the dreaded results of a blood test or x-ray. Once I began researching the subject of pet fish, I discovered there are clubs to join, books to study, and equipment to buy. There are freshwater aquariums and there are saltwater aquariums. For the beginner there is much to learn about selecting fish, selecting plants, how to properly clean the tank, and what it takes to keep the fish alive and healthy.

For those interested in a hobby of fish keeping, it is important to start by determining what kinds of fish you want. This is an important first step because it will determine the size of the aquarium you will need and the equipment you should purchase. In terms of size, 1" of a healthy mature fish per gallon of water is the rule for small fish and more for larger or particularly messy fish. Marine fish will require even more space and water. It is wise to start with a book about the fish you want to keep. The book will let you know what conditions your fish will need and it will also help you set up your tank and equipment. Things that maybe important for you and your fish might include the tank, a filter, a heater, gravel for the bottom, decorations and hiding places for the fish, a top/cover, a stand, and of course the fish.

It is a good practice to set up your tank, fill it with water, and let it run for a couple of days before adding any fish. This way you will be sure that everything is working properly and there are no leaks. Select a few starter fish that are hardy, inexpensive, and small. These fish will not grow much for the first 4-8 weeks. Over these 4-8 weeks you need to be careful about tank maintenance, be sure not to overfeed your starter fish and watch their behavior closely. Do not add any more fish until after these first 4-8 weeks.

Feed and observe your starter fish daily. Regularly check the filters, hoses, fittings, clamps, cords, and lights. Once you get used to it, this should only take a few minutes each day. Every week you will want to perform a 10-15% water change and scrub for algae. These actions should help keep the starter fish healthy. Once you feel confident that everything is working properly and you have become accustomed to the routine, you can begin adding fish that are compatible with each other and your tank.

By the way, an air pump, water pump, and lights are not necessary to keep your fish healthy, but they will make your tank more aesthetically pleasing. In addition, chemicals, a timer, and gravel vacuum or siphon are not necessary, but they make it easier to clean your tank.

So if you want a pet you do not have to walk twice a day, a pet that will not anger your landlady, a pet that does not shed (all four of mine are shedding like mad these days), or if you want a pet that does not make too much noise for your neighbors, you might be the perfect candidate for a fish aquarium. Take a trip to the pet shop and look at the many varieties of beautiful and exotic fish that can add beauty to your home and bring a sense of Zen-like calm to your family. OK, maybe that is too much to expect, but perhaps there will be a few moments of Zen-like calm each day. Happy fishing!

## Vida and Old Age
(July 23, 2010)

Jill tells me that when she is out with Moses, some people get a concerned look on their face and then they ask her if I am still around. Yes, I am still here. To prove it, I am writing this week's column. The theme of my column is "getting old is a real B _ _ _ _ !!!" And I don't mean a female dog.

I am twelve and a half years old. If you use the formula of one year in a human's life equals seven years of a dog's life, the math is 7x 12.5= 87.5. Wow, I AM old. Eighty-seven and a half years old is *really* old. No wonder all my joints hurt when I get up or sit down. No wonder my muzzle is getting white and my eyes are getting cloudy. No wonder I get confused and a little panicked at times. No wonder Jill retired me last year and let Moses take over the job of being her service dog. Heck, how did this happen? One minute I am an awkward puppy fighting my siblings for our mom's milk, and the next thing I know I am old and getting older all the time.

Jill understands all this. She is getting old too. In fact, we both are retired from our jobs and are trying to enjoy these so-called golden years. Yes, we gained wisdom, but other than that, getting old is no fun. That popular saying, "getting old is not for sissies," is so true. I find myself sleeping a lot and getting short of breath after only a quick walk. When I was younger, Jill and I went for 45 minute walks every day. She would turn up her power chair and I would run by her side. We had lots of fun doing this. Now Moses runs by Jill's side.

Do not get me wrong; I am glad Moses took over because it was getting to be too much for me. Now Jill only takes me for a leisurely walk around the neighborhood. These afternoon walks may be 15 minutes or less depending on the heat or the cold. When the weather is too hot or too cold we just skip it. I guess that is one of the advantages of being retired. I even let Moses go with Jill to the YMCA for her morning swim while I sleep in.

Moses has taken over the play stuff too. When Jill or Steve tosses the ball or a stick he goes for it. Unfortunately he still does not get that he has to bring the object back and give it to Jill or Steve for the game to continue. He is a smart boy but this concept seems to be beyond him. I keep telling him to give the object back so they can throw it again. He does not listen, and tries to play keep-away rather than fetch. Oh well, he is still young. Maybe one of these days he will get it.

I am getting tired of writing now. It is time for another snooze. One last thing I must say before signing off—remember never leave your dog(s) in the car even for a minute and even with the windows cracked. In this summer heat your dog(s) could die pretty quickly and that would be very sad. Those are my closing words of wisdom. Oh my, I forgot (senior moment) one other thing: be sure your dogs have fresh water available all the time. That's it for . . . . . . [Soft snoring sounds are coming from Vida and she makes a few twitches and leg movements as she happily dreams of her youth running alongside Jill].

## Search and Rescue Dogs
(July 30, 2010)

"These things we do ... that others may live"

Have you ever wondered about the beautiful, confident, and strong search and rescue (SAR) dogs that you might have seen on an evening news clip? Have you ever wondered how these dogs find missing people lost in wilderness areas like the Adirondack Mountains or a disaster zone like the earthquake in Haiti? Who trains these dogs? What makes them K-9 heroes? To learn more about SAR dogs, I contacted the American Rescue Dog Association and the Adirondack Rescue Dog Association. Here is what I learned:

The American Rescue Dog Association (ARDA) is a national organization for SAR dogs and their handlers. These SAR units work with local law enforcement and other service agencies to assist in finding missing persons. The dog/handler units are specially trained to search for people in wilderness, disasters, and water missions. These units are available 24-hours a day to respond to requests from local, state or federal agencies.

ARDA was founded in 1972. It is the oldest air-scenting search dog organization in the country. The air-scenting SAR dog is trained to locate the scent of ANY human in a specific search area. The dog is not restricted to a missing person's track and can search long after the track is obliterated. Some examples of missions involving ARDA members and their air-scenting dogs include

Jan. 2010   Earthquake in Haiti

Aug. 2005   Hurricane Katrina

Feb. 2003   Space Shuttle Columbia Disaster

Sept. 2001   World Trade Center Attacks

Sept. 2001   Pentagon Attacks

Aug. 1998   Embassy Bombing, Nairobi, Kenya

April 1995   Oklahoma City Bombing

For many of these missions, the SAR units participated in the "sector search" method, a technique using multiple dog/handler teams simultaneously to cover a given area. A search boss coordinates the teams that will work downwind of the assigned sections.

The breeds that excel in SAR work include the German Shepherd, Labrador Retriever, Border Collie, Belgian Mallinois, and the Golden Retriever. Nevertheless, other breeds and mixed breeds have made successful SAR dogs as long as they have excellent scenting abilities and strong prey, pack, and play drives. They must also be stable, friendly and socialized to humans and other dogs. In addition, strong basic obedience training is imperative.

It typically takes a year or more of training before a dog/handler team is mission-ready. Usually training starts as play with simple reward-based exercises. The handler might run and hide a short distance away from the dog. When the dog finds the handler, he is rewarded with a treat, praise or a tug game with a favorite toy. Over time the distance and duration increases and the hide and seek game gets more challenging.

Practice with an agility course is also helpful training for future SAR dogs. The agility courses require the dogs to climb structures, jump through hoops, run through tunnels, and weave in and out of narrow spaces.

Closer to home, the Adirondack Rescue Dog Association, once affiliated with ARDA, is led by Marilyn Greene of Schenectady. Greene has spent over 40 years as a licensed private investigator, SAR handler, and SAR instructor. She kindly answered my questions and shared newspaper articles about her SAR work over the years. One of the first things she told me is that often the search ends with dogs finding a lifeless body. In other words, this work is not for the faint of heart.

When I asked Ms. Greene about her dogs she told me although she has tried working with other breeds, in her forty years as a SAR handler, she finds her German Shepherd dogs have been the best dogs for SAR work. She says they learn faster, can work in a wide range of environments, and can do so for longer periods of time. Her German Shepherds have the necessary endurance. Her current German Shepherd dog is Buddy.

Generally Ms. Greene and her Shepherd come on the scene after a big search has failed to find the missing person. Greene's experience enables her field effectiveness rate (FER) to be as high as 80%. Even before she searches, Ms. Greene looks for similar cases from the past and considers the behavior of previously lost persons. All this information helps her plan the most promising areas for her search.

With a sense of smell far more powerful than a human's and an ability to probe nooks and crannies that humans cannot penetrate, SAR dogs save lives or bring closure and comfort to the families whose friends and relatives succumbed to tragedy. That is what makes SAR dogs and their handlers true heroes.

## Feral Cats and Kittens
(Aug. 6, 2010)

A feral cat is an undomesticated cat. They are wild and will avoid any human contact. Living in colonies within warehouses, barns, and alleyways behind restaurants or grocery stores, feral cats were born outside and never lived as family pets, or they were once a pet but became strays. Over time the stray cats that survive, some simply abandoned by their humans, adapt to living outside with little or no human contact.

When pet cats are forced to fend for themselves outdoors, most die from exposure or accidents. Those that live turn feral and if they have not been sterilized will give birth to feral kittens. These cats and their kittens form feral cat colonies. A pair of breeding cats, producing two or more litters per year, can exponentially have 420,000 offspring over a seven-year period. In response to this staggering problem, volunteer organizations like Alley Cat Allies (ACA) trap, spay/neuter, and return them to their feral colonies.

While still controversial, the ACA and other organizations with similar methods and goals argue that the trap-neuter-release approach is the single most successful method of stabilizing and maintaining healthy feral cat colonies while ensuring the best life for the animals themselves. These organizations claim that trapping, sterilizing and releasing feral cats stabilizes the population at manageable levels, is humane and fosters community compassion, and is more effective and less costly than traditional repeated attempts at extermination.

The traditional practices for reducing the feral cat populations have been by rounding them up, removing them, and taking them to a shelter to be destroyed. Advocates of the trap/neuter/release programs argue that the traditional way only enables other feral cats to soon fill the newly vacated niche and start the breeding process over again. They also state that it is a myth that feral cats lead such short, miserable lives that it is best to trap and destroy them. Further they argue it is also a myth that feral cats are diseased and can make children sick, while in reality feral cats are often as healthy as domestic cats and do not want to interact with children anyway.

Feral cats live anywhere they can find scraps of food and a bit of shelter. Tens of millions now live in the U.S. While stray cats can often be re-socialized and adopted, adult feral cats usually cannot be socialized and will not adjust to living indoors with a human family. In other words, feral is not just another word for stray. The differences are feral cats have a home outdoors and a stray has lost his home. A feral cat wants nothing to do with humans while strays and the kittens of feral cats (if trapped by ten weeks of age) can be socialized and adopted. A stray may become a feral cat if it can learn to survive without humans.

Adult feral cats that end up in shelters are usually deemed unadoptable and are euthanized. Bringing feral cats to most shelters is the same as a death sentence. At least our county shelter has a program that encourages rural farm families with barns to take some feral cats to help control mice and other rodents.

What can you do to help feral cats? Visit the ACA website, www.alleycat.org to find out ways to help stop the killing of feral cats and to promote humane, non-lethal methods of population control. Further, make sure your own pet cats are spayed and neutered, and never abandon a pet. These suggestions are more reflective of a caring society where every life is considered precious.

To summarize, ACA lists five things they want people to know about the feral cat issue.

- Stray and feral cats can live anywhere they find food and shelter.

- "Feral" and "stray" are not the same. Strays can usually be adopted; feral cats usually cannot.

- Kittens of feral cats can be socialized and adopted if the process begins when they are only ten weeks old.

- Studies show feral cats can be as healthy as domestic cats.

- Feral cats avoid human contact. They do not want to interact with you or your children.

ACA advocates Trap-Neuter-Return (TNR)

## Keeping a Trained Dog Trained (Keeping a Good Dog Good)
(Aug. 13, 2010)

Regular readers of this column know about my service dog, Moses. He and I graduated together from the Canine Companions for Independence (CCI) last November. Before I even met Moses, he had been through almost two years of service dog training. Then I was invited to the CCI training center on Long Island so I could learn how to be a service dog handler. I was there for two weeks of intensive training. It has now been nine months since I brought Moses home and we began working together here in Saratoga. He is a wonderful dog that helps me every day. Nevertheless, recently I discovered that to keep Moses at his best we must periodically get back to the basics.

My first hint that things were not going as they should was when I called Moses to come from our back yard to our kitchen door. Instead of running gleefully to the door, he looked up and then continued sniffing weeds at the back fence. I called him again and he just ignored me. After my third call, he looked up and came, but he did so slowly.

Next when I took him with me to the YMCA for my morning swim, I told him to "push" as I gestured to the button that opens the heavy front doors. Instead of jumping up and pushing the button with his nose, he slowly stretched his body long with his rump in the air, his tail wagging and his front paws out next to his nose. Then he gave me a look that seemed to say, "Do I really have to do that? I'd rather sleep or play."

The final act that made me realize he was slipping in his training, was when I dropped my keys with my arms full of books and I said "Moses get." He picked them up for a moment and then decided the metal tasted bad and dropped them back on the ground. The second time I said, "get" he did as he had been taught, but waited for me to grab them instead of putting them on my lap. In other words, he was doing as he was told, but he was slow and it took more than one request. For a service dog, this is getting sloppy.

When one of his trainers gave me a call to see how things were going, I told her about these little slips. She asked me lots of questions about his new life with me. When I told her I was having a hard time telling people not to pet him when he was working, she explained that when other people pet and fuss over him, he gets distracted from his job. He even can get confused about who is his boss or pack leader. So I promised to be more vigilant about asking people not to pet him when he is wearing his work vest. She also said I needed to get him back to the basics of his training.

Within two days, Moses was back on track. Most people understood when I explained that I could not let them distract him from his job as my service dog. Further, Moses and I worked on his recall until it again became instant. After all, a quick recall response could save his life in a dangerous situation. I would be devastated if something happened to him, not only because I have come to love him, but also because of all the people that worked hard to make him the terrific service dog he is.

It is not just service dogs that need to be reminded regularly of their training. A pet that comes when called, stays when told to stay, and walks easily on a loose leash, has been trained successfully in the most important ways. All the other commands used in dog training are only important if you plan to enter your pet in an obedience trial or dog show. The recall and stay are important for a pet's safety. Mastering the walk on a loose leash is important for both the dog and owner so they can share enjoyable walks together. There is nothing worse than a dog that pulls so hard he drags his owner along and chokes himself in the process.

In short, a trained pet dog is a good dog and a safe dog. Obedience training will not turn your dog into a little robot. Rather, with some training he will be a better companion. If he is trained with other dogs, he also will be a socialized dog that will behave even when other dogs are present. For both a service dog and a pet dog, training is essential and repetition of that training is a must or all that good work becomes sloppy or even forgotten.

## Is the Saratoga County Shelter A "No-Kill" Shelter?
(Sept. 17, 2010)

According to Dan Butler, our county shelter supervisor, this is one of the most frequently asked questions at the shelter. It is also one of the most sensitive and emotionally charged questions. Euthanasia is a topic that can challenge our core values and our religious beliefs. No one wants to hear that an animal was "put down" and yet there are situations, as a full service county shelter, where it is a legal obligation to euthanize an animal. On the other hand, according to our county shelter staff and volunteers, the Saratoga County Animal Shelter is a shelter that does everything in its power to avoid euthanasia.

## Difficult situations that require our county shelter to humanely perform euthanasia:

- When an animal has been determined to be a danger to our citizens or has been ordered by a judge to be humanely euthanized
- When an animal has suffered irreparable physical and/or emotional damage due to animal hoarding, neglect or abuse
- When an animal has contracted rabies or another highly contagious disease that threatens the health of other shelter animals and our staff
- When the population of homeless animals exceeds the shelter staff's ability to properly care for them and all other avenues have been exhausted

In response to the first three reasons listed above, the shelter tries to educate people so their animals do not become a danger, do not suffer from mistreatment, and are kept healthy. These efforts include informational pamphlets, advice posted on the county shelter website, and articles in my Whiskers and Tales column. The county shelter's actions regarding the final point listed above are to encourage all pet owners to spay and neuter their pets and to make the animals in the shelter as adoptable as possible. Here are some of the ways they accomplish this:

The shelter accepts help from Friends of the Saratoga County Animal Shelter, H.O.P.E. (Homes For Orphaned Animals Exist), and Mohawk Honda of Schenectady, along with veterinarians who cut their regular fees so shelter animals can receive surgical and other kinds of costly medical care that ultimately makes them more adoptable.

The shelter has helped a group of energetic volunteers establish the cat annex at Clifton Park Center Mall. Since the annex opened last year, over 600 cats and kittens have been adopted from there.

The shelter encourages other volunteers to groom or play or walk shelter animals as a way of socializing them to human attention.

The shelter asks me as a volunteer to writes a pet column for *Saratoga Today* and to regularly feature six shelter animals available for adoption.

The shelter cooperates with television station WTEN on the fourth Monday of every month when they feature one of our animals available for adoption.

The shelter contacts rescue organizations, such as the Capital District Humane Association, Peppertree, Estherville Animal Shelter, and H.O.P.E. We also contact organizations that take specific breeds of cats or dogs.

The shelter has recently opened the new shelter facilities that has more space to house homeless animals, sterile medical facility, more opportunities for volunteers, and areas for prospective adopters to interact with an animal they are considering for adoption.

Remember that no birth is the first step to no-kill.

Please Spay and Neuter Your Pets

## Friends Benefit
(Oct. 29, 2010)

The Benefit Event held last October 7 was a terrific success. Over 300 people attended and Friends of the Saratoga County Animal Shelter (FSCAS) cleared over $20,000. This money will go toward the medical needs of homeless shelter animals in our county. FSCAS is a non-profit organization dedicated to our county animal shelter as a humane haven for animals in crisis. Unlike private shelters (some with impressive endowments), a county animal shelter is totally dependant upon money allocated by elected county officials, the county taxpayers, and occasional donors. And this is where FSCAS comes into action. This volunteer association is the fundraising arm of the shelter.

It is through the Friends' fundraising efforts that shelter animals can receive costly medical attention. To raise money for veterinary costs, FSCAS hosts several benefit events each year. The annual Oct. event is their largest benefit and silent auction, held at the elegant Saratoga National Golf Club. It is open to the public and has proven to be a wonderful affair for individuals and families who want to do something to help the animals. It is the major event for FSCAS, for the Saratoga County Animal Shelter, and most importantly for the animals.

The FSCAS' mission is to work closely with the shelter to identify and meet the needs of the animals in shelter care. This can be as small as providing soft cat beds so every cat has a bed in the shelter that will go with them to their new home after adoption, or providing every dog with a durable chew toy to reduce stress. It can also be as complicated as getting a shelter animal surgery that will make that animal well and more adoptable.

FSCAS has also supported shelter employees who want to be exposed to the newest ideas about animal shelter care. With FSCAS' help several shelter employees have attended some of these national conferences and workshops.

Providing pet food to the local food bank so pet owners in our county can care for their pets through difficult economic times is another way FSCAS has helped our county animals from time to time. Hopefully pet food in the food bank will keep owners from having to make the difficult decision to surrender their pets because they can no longer afford to feed them.

Friends of the Saratoga County Animal Shelter also work to let residents know about the county shelter as a place to go when looking for a new pet. Members hand out information about the shelter and animal care at dog walks, county fairs, and other events.

## Grand Opening of the New County Shelter
(Nov. 12, 2010)

Last Saturday was the grand opening of the new Saratoga County Animal Shelter. It marks the culmination of years of careful planning and vision. It symbolizes a new day for the homeless, neglected, abused, and lost animals in our county. The grand opening also reflects well on a county that cares about its domesticated animals and recognizes that these animals depend on humans for protection and shelter and in return they give companionship and unconditional love.

So many people came to the grand opening, at one point Moses and I had to escape out the front door. There just was not enough room for my wheelchair and Moses' long body and wagging tail. By gently nosing the backs of people's legs Moses moved people aside (parting the sea?) so we could pass. Actually our timing was perfect because just as we reached the door, it was announced that everyone should go outside for the ribbon cutting. The group, including cameramen for local news stations, photographers snapping stills, county and state dignitaries, and many citizens that care about animals, poured out of the building that looks like a new red barn.

Dan Butler, the animal shelter supervisor spoke outside about all the challenges, victories, difficulties and rewards that made up the process of getting the new shelter built. He thanked the many individuals and organizations that helped make the new shelter a reality. He was particularly grateful for the support of the county supervisors who believed in the project. Amazingly, once ground was broken, this project took only one year to complete and it came in under budget. How many other large public projects can say this?

After Dan introduced several other speakers it was time for the ribbon cutting. When the deed was done, the crowd cheered and clapped. But it was pretty cold outside so most did not waste too much time returning to the warmth of the building. Back inside there were balloons, hot dogs, pies, and coffee.

I stayed out front to show my husband Steve all the memorial bricks leading up to the entrance. I wanted to surprise him because I purchased one in honor of his beloved German shepherd that passed away several years ago. I also purchased a brick with the names of our current pets; Vida, Moses, and our cats, Sully and Magic.

At the Grand Opening, Moses and I ran into several regular readers of "Whiskers and Tales." It is always fun to chat with these folks. I love to hear about their pets. At the event, one regular reader told me a great story about a cat she adopted. The cat had issues, kept her distance and acted almost like a feral cat. One day the woman was sick. She lay on the couch feeling miserable. Then she said to the cat, "I wish you were a lap cat." The cat approached the woman for the first time, curled up on her lap, and stayed there. Ever since this incident the cat has become less timid, and regularly finds a lap to warm.

With Moses at my side, talking to people is easy. At one point I struck up a conversation with state Senator Roy MacDonald. He talked about his family and the pets he had as a kid. During our conversation lots of people came up to him to say a few words. He was a master at turning to them for an exchange and then turning back to me, picking up our conversation exactly where we left off. He never skipped a beat. This must be one of those skills he learned after years in public office. I kept thinking how he seems to be a genuinely nice man. At the end of our conversation, we agreed that the new Saratoga County Animal Shelter is surely the finest shelter in the East and it will be the model shelter for many years to come.

## Boo and Pets That Escape
(Nov. 24, 2010)

Years ago I had a funny spayed female Beagle named Boo. She was a character and a good buddy when I was going through a difficult time. My only complaint about Boo was her insatiable appetite for food. If it was slightly rotten food, from Boo's perspective it was all the better. She somehow knew when the garbage went out in our neighborhood and she would slip out of the yard and go scrounging in the garbage.

One Thanksgiving Boo pulled an entire turkey carcass from the trash and apparently ate every last bone. I found her on the back porch lying on her back with a huge tummy. The veterinarian said I should wait and see if she gets sick. Amazingly Boo digested the whole thing without even a belch.

I was lucky that Boo did not get a splintered bone struck in her intestines. I was also lucky that when Boo found a way out of our yard she always came back in one piece. After many fence repairs and keeping an eye on her every trash day, I finally was able to have peace of mind regarding Boo.

Dogs and indoor cats do manage to get away at times, even when the owner has taken all precautions to avoid the loss of a pet. It is important to know what to do should your beloved pet take off.

## What to do if you lose your pet?

If your dog gets out of your backyard or if your indoor cat slips out a door left ajar, there are things you can do to better your chances of reuniting with them. Even if you have an outdoor cat that fails to return home one day, there are things you can do to optimize the likelihood of retrieving them.

- Always keep your pet identified. This can be done in many ways, some are more or less expensive than other ways, but whatever method you choose, be sure that if someone finds your lost pet, they can contact you. Forms of pet identification include a current dog license tag, vaccination tags, personal identification tags, or a microchip tag. These are all ways for your pet to be identified. Since ID tags can come off and get lost in the brush, another way to identify your pet is with a personalized collar. These collars can be stitched with your dog's name and your phone number. These collars are available through pet supply and hunting catalogues.
- Keep available a current photo, especially one that shows any distinguishing markings.
- Contact all animal control officers, animal shelters, and veterinarians in the area.
- Place a lost pet ad in the local newspapers and scan the found ads daily. Many local papers will run 3-7 days of lost and found pet ads for free.
- Place fliers in as many locations as possible and offer a reward.
- Notify your neighbors.
- If the animal is microchipped, notify the organization

where it is registered. Be sure that you keep up on your annual fees for the microchip.
- Call the shelters in your area and check shelter web sites under "strays."

### What to do if you find a lost pet?

- Contact animal control for the town in which the animal was found. If unable to contact an animal control officer call a shelter or local law enforcement.
- Place a free ad in several papers with a description of the animal plus when and where it was found.

Remember, neutered and spayed pets are less likely to roam.

For more information on animal control and a listing of animal control officers in the county go to the Saratoga County Animal Shelter web site www.saratogacountyny.gov.

## Pets and the Upcoming Holidays
(Dec. 17, 2010)

We have all seen the image of a child's delight at discovering a new puppy or kitten under the tree at the holidays. Nevertheless, this cute image is misleading, because the holidays are not the best time to give your child a pet. Typically there is so much chaos with relatives and friends dropping by and excitement expressed by family members over their other gifts that a new dog or cat could feel overwhelmed and frightened. This will not make for an easy transition as the animal might have just left his mother and littermates or his shelter kennel. If these are not reason enough to postpone bringing home a new pet until after the holidays, consider the fact that your child might see the pet as just another new toy.

Children need to learn that the puppy or kitten, unlike a Barbie doll or a shiny red truck, feel pain, hunger, loneliness, and will die if not looked after by a human. Kids need to learn that having a pet is a long-term commitment and a responsibility. The dog needs to walk regularly even when it is cold outside. The cat needs to play often so she does not become overweight and unhealthy. Dogs can live for 14 years or more and cats for 20 years. If a child is too young to understand these things, they are too young to have a kitty or pup.

Too often children lose interest in their pet after a few weeks and if mom or dad does not take over the care of the animal, it could end up in the shelter where it may or may not get a home. One veterinarian told me how it is not uncommon for a client to come in with a perfectly healthy dog or cat and request that the doctor put him down because no one in the family has time to care for him.

If your family already has a pet, there are other things to think about during the holidays. If you have a Christmas tree, be sure it is properly anchored so that it cannot tip over onto your pet below. Also keep the animals out of the tree water, which may contain fertilizers that can cause stomach upsets. Further, kitties love to play with tinsel that if swallowed can obstruct the digestive tract, causing vomiting, dehydration and possibly require surgery. It is best to hang your ornaments high so the pets cannot knock them off the tree and chew on them. After we got our cats, Sully and Magic, my husband Steve discovered some ornaments in the store that were made of non-breakable plastic but looked just like the old glass ones. We put these ornaments on the lower branches and no one could tell the difference.

When it comes to all the rich food we eat at the holidays, be sure not to leave plates of food unattended and keep lids on garbage containers. Some of you will remember my story about my beagle, Boo that ate a whole turkey carcass on Thanksgiving one year. It was my fault because I failed to secure the lid on the garbage container. Surprisingly, Boo survived but was pretty uncomfortable for several hours. Fatty spicy foods, as well as bones are not good for our pets. If you like to give your pet treats and presents, make it an indestructible toy like a Kong smeared with a little bit of peanut butter for your dog and a "fishing stick" with feathers for your cat. The great thing about the fishing stick is that the cat plays interactively with you or your children. While cats also love to play with ribbon or yarn, these can get stuck in their intestines, just like tinsel.

Candles are often central to holiday celebrations; however, be sure not to leave them unattended because pets can burn themselves or tip them over. If I put a candle on our coffee table, it is the perfect height for our dog Moses to whack it with his tail. All candles in our house are placed higher than his tail. I also keep an eye on holly, mistletoe, and poinsettias (the least toxic of the three), because they are mildly toxic and if ingested they can cause your pet to experience nausea, vomiting, or diarrhea. Other things your pets should avoid include chocolate, alcoholic drinks, and too much excitement. For the latter, be sure your pets have a quiet refuge with fresh water and a warm place to snuggle.

## Two Pet Peeves at the Spa State Park
(Jan. 7, 2011)

One of my favorite places to take Moses for his daily run is our beautiful Spa State Park. I am always amazed that we have such a special spot in our community. It is so close and yet it feels like it is far away from life in town or in our surrounding neighborhoods. The trees and the sweet smell of the pine needles take me back to wonderful camping trips of my youth growing up in southern California. The main difference is that in California we had to drive hours to get out of the city, whereas here I can drive ten minutes to be among the pines. I can even sit by a brook with my dog Moses and watch the birds while eating my lunch at a picnic table.

Moses and I move through the park together enjoying the peaceful quiet. When he runs, it is by my wheelchair. I set the pace and he gleefully follows, never pulling on the leash. If I slow down he slows down so that he is always by my side. Sometimes it feels like we are one. Nevertheless, this peaceful picture is disrupted when another dog owner decides to let her dog off lead.

There are signs throughout the park about keeping dogs on leash. Nevertheless, some dog owners think this rule does not apply to them. They want to let their dogs run free. I have no argument with this desire, but there are dog parks for that. I am not a big fan of dog parks because owners must be willing to take the risk that a dogfight might erupt. In the case of the impromptu dog park off of Crescent Street, owners also must be willing to take the risk that a dog could run into Route 9 traffic or disappear into the woods to the east or the south. The latter situation happened just last summer.

Getting back to the Spa state park which is NOT a dog park, what really gets our hackles up is when an excited off leash dog comes charging at Moses and me while his owner yells, "Its ok, he's friendly!" Moses is a very calm dog, but he becomes concerned when an unknown dog comes racing straight at him and when he feels me brace myself for the impact, he becomes even more agitated. Our peaceful time together in the park is disrupted and even though I am dog lover, I am left shaken. I can only wonder how a child or an adult who fears dogs might feel in the same situation.

Years ago when we were less experienced with dogs, my husband and I had a Doberman mix named Krieger. He was a dog that was devoted to Steve, overly protective of me, and wary of everyone else. He could be aggressive towards people or other dogs that he considered a threat to either of us. We had to be very careful with him or he would get himself into trouble when he tried to protect us. We took him to the New Skete Monks and they admitted that after three weeks working with him, Krieger would not bond with any of them. He just kept looking for Steve to come back for him. Some of our friends nicknamed Krieger, the Devil Dog. If you have ever had a dog like this, you know it is a grave responsibility keeping everyone safe. When Steve would walk Krieger in the State park he would stay clear of other dogs and people. If another dog owner let their dog off leash and called out to Steve, "Its ok, he's friendly!" he would yell back, "OK, but mine isn't friendly!" Then he would have to muscle Krieger in close and tell the owner of the other dog to grab their free running pet. It was not pleasant for anyone!

So my number one pet peeve in the Spa State Park is when owners let their dogs run off leash. Moving on, my second pet peeve in the Spa Sate Park is when dog owners fail to clean up after their dog. This looks bad for all of us. It assumes that the park grounds crew should stop their mowing or pruning to pick up a nasty pile of poop. The Park people make it so easy for dog owners to do the right thing. There are several stations with receptacles and black plastic bags for owners to carry with them. They even provide instructions on how to pick up the poop with the bag while never soiling the hands. I have even seen where people pick up the poop with the bag, but then leave the bag on the trail rather than taking it to the nearest receptacle.

To show our appreciation for the marvelous park we have in our community where we can take our dogs, let's follow the rules that make it a better place for everyone.

Let's not give the state any reasons to exclude our four-legged best friends.

## In Memory of Vida (1998-2011)
(Feb. 4, 2011)

Those of you who have read my column since the beginning know about my first service dog, Vida. I named her Vida (pronounced VEEDA) because it means "life" in Spanish and she brought me a new approach to life after I had become increasingly affected by Multiple Sclerosis. That was eleven years ago and Vida has been there to help me ever since. When she reached 12 years old, I retired her from service dog duties, but she stayed with me as a pet. My new service dog Moses took over her work and the two of them along with our cats, Sully and Magic, became our family.

At 13 years old Vida's black fur was grey around her muzzle but she still loved meal times and she always was eager to go for a slow afternoon walk with my husband, Steve or with me in my wheelchair. Once in a while when I would drop a glove, she would pick it up for me like she did in her earlier years. She never forgot things I taught her, but she began to suffer from a bit of doggy dementia and arthritis. The dementia resulted in her occasionally getting confused about where she was or what she was doing. For example, she would go outside and become lost about how to get off the deck and onto the lawn or vice versa. Further, the arthritis progressed until it was hard for her to get up from a down position, and it became clear that she was in some pain.

One of the hardest moments for any dog or cat lover is when making the decision to humanely help a pet pass.

Thankfully, Vida made this relatively easy for me. One day she was out for her walk in the State Park with Steve, and the next morning she simply could not get up at all. She refused to eat anything and she calmly looked at me in a way that said she was ready. I called our vet and we took her right over. The doctor checked her over carefully. All four of her legs and her tail were nearly motionless. It was clear to all of us that it was time to say good-bye to Vida. Her passing was peaceful and sweet. She was calm and even seemed grateful. I cried some, but I knew she had lived a good life and she had been devoted to me through good times and bad. She was a very good girl and we will miss her presence for years to come.

When I think back on her life with me I remember how Vida would come to class when I taught anthropology at Skidmore College. She would sit beside me as I lectured. At some point she would slide down, rest her chin on her paws, and close her eyes. A little bit later she would start to softly snore. This would cause the students to laugh and some would quietly whisper to each other that they also felt like napping. I would take all this as a not-so-subtle hint the lecture was getting boring. Sometimes, rather than snore, Vida would just let out a groan and that also would break up the class. Once class was over and a few students crowded around me to ask about an assignment or a point they did not understand in the reading, Vida would quietly leave the room with the other students. She would move with the crowd out of the building and over to the dining hall, following the smell of the hamburgers cooking. Like most labs, she was always hungry.

When Skidmore's President Philip Glotzbach took office in 2003, Vida and I stood in line to meet him. He shook my hand and then asked if he could give Vida a pat on her head. I said sure and just as he reached down a reporter snapped a picture. It was a wonderful moment caught on film. My academic department had it blown up to poster size and hung it in the department office. Vida had become something of a Sociology, Anthropology, and Social Work mascot with that photograph.

Vida flew with me to California several times and once to Chicago. She also went with Steve and me on car trips throughout New England. She was a good traveler and had been quick to learn how to walk by my wheelchair without getting too close, lagging behind or moving out too far in front. She knew to stay right by my left side. Vida was the first dog I successfully trained with the help of professional dog trainer, Michelle Dudley of Glens Falls' Top Dog. Vida was also the first dog I took everywhere with me. Spending that much time with a dog teaches one how to read the dog's every need and the dog in turn learns how to anticipate a handler's every move.

The evening after we said our good-byes to Vida, Moses looked for her all over the house. They never were very chummy because Vida did not want to play with the younger Moses, but he respected her and seemed to help her when she would become confused or fearful of going out. He would lead the way and she would follow his more confidant strides.

In closing, if there is an afterlife, I know Vida will be waiting patiently for me to come give her a biscuit, a hug, and take her for a run. It will be a run without the aches and pains of old age or the confusion from dementia, and for me, it will be a run without the need of a wheelchair!

## Greyhounds and Dog Racing
(March 18 2011)

The other day, my Black Lab, Moses and I took our daily walk. This time we went downtown instead of taking our usual mile or more in the state park. Going downtown is always fun because there is a different energy. Rather than focusing on squirrels, birds and trees, a walk downtown means lots of people, cars, excitement and action. My preference is the park, but occasional walks in town are fun too. On this walk, we came across a blond woman walking her two retired Greyhounds along Broadway. These beautiful and noble looking creatures with their long legs, narrow heads, slender bodies and gentle eyes fascinated Moses. While the woman and I talked briefly about our dogs, Moses and the two Greyhounds, named Chase and Dodger, had their own conversation.

As Moses and I moved along, he was full of questions about Greyhounds and dog racing. I tried to answer his questions. At first he thought being a racing dog would be lots of fun, but when I explained to him about the problems of organized dog racing, he felt sorry for Ggreyhounds and his new friends, Chase and Dodger. I told him that Chase and Dodger were two of the lucky ones because after they were retired from racing, they were rescued by one of the non-profit Greyhound rescue organizations and successfully adopted into a forever home. I said many more Greyhounds are not so lucky. Moses wanted to know more and this is what I told him:

According to the Humane Society of the United States, in 2000, an estimated 19,000 Greyhounds were killed. This includes 7,600 Greyhound puppies that were culled because they were not considered promising racers, and another 11,400 retirees that were not rescued and adopted. Other Greyhounds no longer useful to the dog racing industry were sold to research labs or sent to foreign racetracks where track conditions can be deplorable.

Because the goal of dog racing is to generate income, the industry depends on a breeding surplus so only the fastest dogs are raced and then raced only as long as they continue to win. A dog's racing career is typically 3-4 years. In contrast, if able to live out his or her full life as a companion dog, a Greyhound can live to be 13 years or more.

During the 1990s seven states banned dog racing: Idaho, Maine, North Carolina, Nevada, Vermont, Virginia and Washington. There are currently tracks operating in Alabama, Arkansas, Arizona, Iowa, Rhode Island, Texas, Florida, West Virginia, and Wisconsin. Unfortunately, the federal Animal Welfare Act does not oversee these states' handling of the dog racing industry.

Moses thanked me for the rundown on Greyhounds and racing. He said Chase and Dodger told him they had fond memories of their race days, but he agreed it was good that the nice blond lady adopted them so they can relax and enjoy their retirement.

If any of my readers want to know more about adopting retired Greyhounds they might look into a local not-for-profit organization called Forever Home Greyhound Adoptions. This organization provides important information on adopting a retired Greyhound. They do not dwell on the negative aspects of dog racing but rather focus their energies on finding good homes for Greyhounds and act to build a workable relationship with the racing industry. Further, they educate potential adopters about issues particular to Greyhounds. For example, they explain why Greyhounds must never be off a leash, why some Greyhounds do not do well with cats, or why a fenced-in yard is so important. They are a very well organized group that sets up situations where people can see and interact with the Greyhounds available for adoption. They are also very careful that their Greyhounds go to a responsible owner in a loving home environment. If you want to know more about adopting a Greyhound or would like to help Greyhounds by volunteering time or donating financial support, see the website at www.foreverhomegreyhounds.com. If you do not use the web, call (518) 261-7025.

## Traveling to New Hampshire With Moses
(April 29, 2011)

Some of you may remember how my Canine Companions for Independence (CCI) service dog, Moses has to periodically be retested for his public access permit. This past week my husband and I took him for that recertification test. Thankfully we didn't have to go to the CCI training center on Long Island. I say thankfully because the traffic and driving on Long Island can be such a nightmare. No, this time we had the much more inviting option of going to a community center in Dover, New Hampshire.

For weeks I knew this test was coming up and I knew that Moses would be fine because we practice all his commands for 10-15 minutes almost every day before we start our mile to two-mile runs where I turn up the speed on my motorized wheelchair and he trots alongside me. Nevertheless, as the time got closer I worried about the test. Unfortunately, I am a worrier by nature. I fret over too many things in life. It is to the point that I think if I don't worry and fret before something like an exam, I will fail. I know worry is usually just a waste of energy, but old habits are hard to break. This time was going to be different, I told myself. This time I was going to be calm—calm like Moses. I was going to learn from him. Nothing was going to get me in a panic this time. Moses and I were going to sail through this hurdle.

As I was packing for the trip, I came across a 2009 notebook from my two weeks at CCI when I was learning how to work with Moses. I started looking over my notes and then I saw it. I had written it down in red ink and underlined it twice. As an adult dog Moses should weigh between 69 and 73 lbs. Then my notes were full of warnings about potential health problems if you let your dog become overweight. Gulp! The vet just weighed him a week ago and he weighed 75 lbs. She said he looked good, but after seeing the ideal weight figures in my notebook, I began to worry. My mind started playing tricks on me. I looked at Moses and suddenly he looked fat!

I told my husband, Steve and he said, "get a grip." He got me to think it through and I became calmer. What is the worst thing that could happen? They could tell me to cut down on his food. After an hour or so I "got a grip" and began to relax about his weight.

Our trip to New Hampshire began beautifully. The sun was shining, in the car we played favorite old tunes on the CD player, and we talked about all kinds of things. The drive across Vermont was beautiful. We stopped twice to let Moses stretch his legs and relieve himself. We carried plenty of fresh water for him, but when he is stuck in a car or an airplane, he won't drink any water until he is sure he will get a chance to "water" a patch of grass. I learned this about him when we few out to California in 2010 and because we almost missed our connection, for ten straight hours there was no place for him to relieve himself. Throughout the time all he would take in terms of liquid were a few ice chips to wet his mouth. Even without losing the planned break between flights, finding a patch of grass in an airport can be quiet a challenge.

Since that California trip, I learned that in 2009 the Department of Transportation instructed all airlines and airports to collaborate on creating relief areas for pets and service dogs. Some airports took the mandate more seriously than others. The Atlanta airport really went all out. On November 18, 2009, they opened an off-leash dog park. This fully-fenced facility features flowers, grass, rocks, benches and two original pieces of art for the dogs to enjoy (can you believe this?). Of course biodegradable bags to clean up waste are available. For more information on dog friendly airports and relief areas, see www.petfriendlytravel.com/airports. But I have digressed. Back to our car trip to Dover.

After we found the Dover motel and checked in to our room, we fed Moses and then we went out to dinner. The waitress hadn't seen us come in so when we were getting ready to leave after a lovely meal, I guided Moses out from under our table and she was startled. He had been so good throughout dinner our waitress didn't even realize he was there. The CCI people would have been proud of Moses.

The next day was test day. We had to be at the community center by 5 pm. I was feeling relaxed and confident that Moses and I were ready to shine. Steve agreed to get us there by 4:30 just to be on the safe side. He even went over earlier to be sure he knew where to go. We were supposed to meet in the parking lot. We sat in our car looking for other people with CCI dogs, but there were none. We were early, but I thought there should be some others waiting. At 4:45, I began to worry that I got the time wrong. I called the cell phone of the woman who was to give the test, but there was no answer. Then I started to think the time was 5:30, but I told Steve 5 pm so we were sure to be early. Suddenly a woman and a dog with a CCI vest came around the building from the other side. I asked her if she was there for the test and she said, yes they had just finished!

All my efforts to stay calm went out the window as I realized something was very wrong. The woman said we should hurry because they were just finishing up. Apparently they began the testing at 4:30! I went into a panic as Steve drove us around to the front of the building. I got out with Moses and tore into the place. They examiner said hurry because they were about to close up the building. I don't remember much after that.

As if in a dream-state I put Moses through the tasks the examiner requested. "Have him pick up the pen and give it to you…Put him in a down stay and walk away around the corner…Have him stand so I can look at his teeth, nails, coat, and musculature…load him into the elevator safely… put him in a sit-stay while I toss kibble at his feet…

She smiled and said we passed and that a new three-year certificate would come in the mail. She did ask if he had put on a little winter weight, but she didn't make a big deal about it. Later when I asked Steve, he said Moses did everything she asked of us. He said Moses was calm even though I had just lost my cool when faced with the fact that I had the time wrong and we might have missed the whole exam!

Will I ever learn not to fret? Will I ever learn to be calm like my Moses? Will I ever trust that things will work out one way or another, with or without worry? Maybe if I can learn from Moses I will one day be free from years of worrying and become more like him and his calm demeanor.

## Blessing of the Animals
(July 22, 2011)

When I was a kid, I went with my family to an Episcopal church in North Hollywood most Sundays. I went until

I was 13 years old, confirmed and allowed to take Holy Communion. I promised my mother I would go to church until I passed through this rite of passage, but then after my first Communion, I never went back. My mother said this was not unusual (I had become a rebellious teenager), but that when I got older I would start going back to church again. Well, I am almost a senior citizen now, and guess what? I went back to church last August and will go again this August. What brought me back was a service devoted to the Blessing of the Animals. It was held at the Unitarian Universalist Congregation of Saratoga Springs.

I really enjoyed the service last year. People brought dogs, cats in carriers, and even reptile pets. Amazingly, it seemed that the animals knew they were in church and were quiet and attentive. I brought Moses and my friend Sandy. Sandy, who is the President of the Friends of the Saratoga County Animal Shelter, had recently lost her dog Michi to a sudden illness. After Sandy and I joined in and sang some hymns and listened to a reading and a story, the pet remembrance ritual began. Members of the congregation could light a candle and say a few words about a pet they had loved and lost. It was the most moving part of the service. Sandy sat on the bench to my left and Moses sat on the floor at my right. When Sandy quietly shed a few tears thinking about her Michi, Moses pushed past me and put his head on her lap as if to comfort her.

The whole event was lovely and when last year's service leader, Linda Wilkes, asked me to participate in this year's Blessing of the Animals, I said of course. To plan for the service Linda, Nedra Stimpfle, Cynthia Klopfer, and I met at Virgils, a sweet little tea and sandwich shop on Henry Street. The décor reminded me of my grandmother's comfortable sitting room. Nedra, Cynthia and I had our dogs with us. We made our plans for the next Blessing of the Animals service to be held on August 14 at 10 am.

The Unitarian Universalist church is located at 624 N. Broadway, Saratoga Springs. You do not have to be a current member to come to a service. Everyone is invited and well-socialized pets are welcomed too for this special occasion. Now that they have put in a ramp, who knows? I might just start going to church regularly. My dear mother would be pleased about that. But when I was a kid in North Hollywood, I had never heard of a Blessing of the Animals so I thought I would do a bit of research on the topic. This is what I learned:

The Blessing of the Animals is associated with Saint Francis of Assisi who is considered the Patron Saint of animals and of the natural environment, or what we now refer to as the ecology. There are stories about Saint Francis being able to converse with birds. Statues of him usually have birds sitting on his open hands, shoulders and head with other animals curled up at his feet. According to the Catholic calendar, his feast day is October 4th. Because of this, most churches that celebrate the Blessing of the Animals do so on or near this date.

It seems like the Catholic Church, the Church of England, and the Episcopal Church have been practicing the Blessing of the Animals most widely. There are disagreements within these churches and denominations, however, as to the validity or the importance of celebrating the Blessing of the Animals. In fact, some individual priests will not conduct this ritual. In more recent times the practice has appeared in a variety of Protestant churches as well. I also found a reference to a Blessing of the Animals as a new tradition in Judaism. Nevertheless, I could not confirm this claim. In rural areas it is not uncommon for horses, pigs, sheep. or cows to be included in the blessing ceremony. Often times with these larger animals there will be a procession out-of-doors.

If you have an animal you would like to be blessed, or if you would like to light a candle for one that is no longer with you, mark your calendar for Sunday, August 14. Also, after the service Moses and I would love to meet you and your pet.

## Winning Over Joan
(Aug. 12, 2011)

This past week Joan, a very dear friend of mine flew here from her home in New Mexico to visit for ten days. Joan and I have been friends for 37 years. She is a "full-blooded" Pueblo Indian and a resident of Santo Domingo Indian Reservation, located about sixty miles north of Albuquerque and sixty miles south of Santa Fe. She is a special education teacher at the Santo Domingo elementary school and she regularly sews traditional ceremonial Pueblo clothing for members of her village. Joan and I share many memories of adventures in the Southwest as well as our general attitudes about life, but one thing we do not share is our feelings about dogs and cats.

At Joan's village there are plenty of dogs and some cats that serve the purpose of keeping refuse cleaned up and rodents in check. These canines and felines are not treated badly, but they are not seen as pets and they are not brought into the living quarters of the homes. Rather, they are roaming creatures with important outside jobs. For Joan and most of her people these animals are never brought into the house because they are considered unclean. Their jobs of scavenger and hunter go back to prehistoric Pueblo times. Nevertheless Joan tells me, "These days there are a few people in the village who actually keep a dog or a cat as a pet in the house like the White people do, but this is rare and considered a little odd."

Joan's village of Santo Domingo is well known for their elaborate corn dances where hundreds of dancers and singers participate in a large plaza every year on August 4th. Sometimes tourists come to see these incredible events. I have had the pleasure of witnessing many of them. During the dance day, occasionally a tourist will approach a village dog lurking at the edge of the plaza, fuss over the animal and even put their face down for a dog kiss. The Pueblo people watching the dance that notice this tourist behavior see it as pretty disgusting and ask themselves, "Why would anyone want a kiss from the garbage mouth of a flea-bitten mongrel?"

Keeping in mind our different beliefs about the proper place of dogs and cats, it should not come as a surprise that when Joan visited me, she just shook her head and had to look the other way when she saw how my dog, Moses and our cats, Sully and Magic practically have free run of our home. Joan and I recognize that our contrasting attitudes about domesticated canines and felines are a result of historical and cultural differences in our backgrounds and we tease each other about those differences. Moses, however, was determined to impress Joan and win her over during the ten-day visit.

At first Joan ignored Moses. When he came up to her for a pat on the head, she avoided touching him. Moses, who is used to people always making a fuss over him, seemed incredulous that he couldn't charm Joan who also tried to ignore the cats. This was easy with Magic because she is always leery of new people anyway, but Sully was beside himself when she wouldn't play with him. Nevertheless, it wasn't long before Joan began to see why I said Moses was an exceptional dog. Sully, on the other hand, never really won her over, especially after he tried to chew on the tip of her long braid that reaches well below the small of her back.

One of the purposes of Joan's trip was for us to drive to Niagara Falls together. Neither of us had ever seen the falls and my friend and colleague, Michael from my teaching days at Skidmore, offered to be our guide. Michael, Joan, and I piled into my car along with Moses and headed north for our road trip. Joan quietly observed Moses throughout the trip. By the end she simply said, "Moses is a really good dog." This was very high praise from Joan.

What impressed her the most about Moses? Was it that he pressed his nose on handicap buttons to open heavy doors for me? Was it the way he lay down quietly under the table when we ate at restaurants? Did she notice how he paid no attention to other dogs passing us by on the street? Maybe she was impressed by the way he picked up things out of my reach when I told him, "Moses, get." Did she notice how Moses was calm when butterflies landed on his head as we explored a butterfly conservatory or when we boarded the Maid of the Mist and passed near the roaring falls that covered us all in a cool fine mist of water? Perhaps she decided Moses was special when he became concerned if Joan or I left our group and when my wheelchair almost tipped me out onto the pavement when I tried to go down a much too steep ramp.

It was probably all these things. When I dropped Joan off at the airport for her flight back to New Mexico she said to Moses, "Thank you Moses, for looking after us and keep taking care of Jill." I guess Moses did it. He won Joan over. Maybe on her next trip out, Sully will manage to do the same!

# Humans Aiding Animals, Animals Aiding Humans, Part I
(Aug. 26, 2011)

On Aug. 14 at the Unitarian Universalist Congregation of Saratoga Springs, I was invited to be one of two guest speakers during their Blessing of the Animal service. I was to talk about animals helping people and Cynthia Klopfer was to talk about people helping animals. My talk focused on service dogs and my personal experiences with Moses, my CCI dog (Canine Companions for Independence) and Cynthia's talk focused on her many years rescuing and finding loving homes for retired or homeless Greyhound and Italian Greyhound dogs.

For this special service, people brought their pets or pictures of their pets. The service leaders were Nedra Stimpfle and Linda Wilkes who guided the congregation through prayers for animals, stories and songs about animals, and a lovely pet remembrance ritual where anyone could come up front and light a candle for a past or present pet.

The service was both emotionally moving and humorous. For me the most emotionally moving moment was during the pet remembrance ritual when a woman came forward and lit a candle for all the euthanized animals that had no one to mourn their passing. On the other hand, I found the lightest part of the service was when everyone sang a song by Barry Louis Pollisar, titled "Oh I Wanna Be a Dog" followed by "Oh I Wanna be a Cat."

As usual, I was very nervous before I began my part in the service. Even after twenty-five years teaching college students and engaging in related public speaking events, I still get stage fright. Maybe it is because my father and mother who were performers always said when you stop having nerves before you go on, you probably have lost your required edge to do a good job. Whatever the reason, as soon as I begin, I feel relaxed and even enjoy speaking, especially about something that matters to me like animals helping humans.

I began my talk by offering a working definition and a brief discussion of assistance animals: Assistance animals transform the lives of their human partners who have physical and/or mental disabilities by serving as their devoted companion, helper, aide, best friend and close member of the family. They are a perfect example of animals helping humans. Assistance animals are most often dogs, but miniature horses, cats, and even birds have been trained to be an assistance animal.

Assistance dogs include Guide dogs for the blind, Service dogs (like my Moses), Hearing Alert dogs, Seizure Alert dogs, and Medical Alert dogs. These dogs go through training before they can be paired up with a human in need of help. Guide dogs for the blind must learn to safely lead their blind partner even through busy intersections. Service dogs need to learn how to bring out-of-reach objects to their disabled humans. Hearing alert dogs must learn to react to the door bell, the telephone or a fire alarm and signal their human partner. Seizure alert dogs and medical alert dogs are born with an uncanny ability to sense a seizure, a change in blood pressure, or a change in blood sugar levels even before the humans know. Their training involves teaching them ways to effectively alert by barking, whining, or stroking their human partner.

Next I explained that Therapy dogs are not a type of assistance dog because they work with groups rather than with a single disabled human partner. Therapy dogs visit libraries, schools, hospitals, nursing homes, and courtrooms. They must be trained in obedience and good citizenship. They have helped to calm witnesses in court, children learning to read, individuals facing surgery or other frightening medical procedures, and lonely seniors who miss having a pet.

Then I turned from this general information about animals helping humans to the specific example of how my service dog Moses helps me in practical terms, emotional terms, and spiritual terms. To be continued next week.

---

## Humans Aiding Animals, Animals Aiding Humans, Part II
(Sept. 2, 2011)

Last week this column began a two-part description of my invited talk for the Blessing of the Animals service held at the Unitarian Universalist church of Saratoga Springs on Sunday, August 14. In the first half of the talk that was to focus on animals aiding humans, I explained how an assistance animal is trained to be a companion and helper to their disabled human partner. I said most assistance animals are dogs, including guide dogs, service dogs, and medical alert dogs that can help people who are blind, use wheelchairs, or live with medical conditions such as diabetes or epilepsy. Today I will share the second half of the talk where I shift from a general discussion of assistance dogs to particular experiences with Moses, my CCI (Canine Companions for Independence) assistance animal.

When Moses and I encounter people on the street or in a grocery store, restaurant, or the mall, the question most often asked is," What does your dog do for you?" This question is hard for me to answer in a few short sentences because he does so much for me in practical, emotional and spiritual ways.

In practical terms, Moses picks up stuff that I can't reach while I am seated in my wheelchair. For example, there have been several times that I have dropped my keys or let them slip down between the seats of the car. My car is equipped with hand controls, but I still need my keys to get started. All I have to do is point in the direction of the dropped keys and say, "Moses get." He picks them up in his mouth and drops them on my lap or in my hands when I say, "Moses give." When I dropped my keys last winter in the snow, Moses dug deep until he had them in his mouth.

Another example of a practical task Moses does for me involves opening heavy doors when my hands are full. This happens at the YMCA and the mall. I say, "Moses push" and he jumps up and pushes the handicap button with his nose so the door opens for us to enter or exit the building.

One of the most important practical things Moses can do for me is get my cell phone and bring it to me so I can call 911 if I am having a problem. We are still working on this task because I need to remember to leave my cell phone in the same place each day we are home and the same place in my purse when we are out so Moses knows where to look.

Finally, Moses can clear a path for my wheelchair. This often means he has to pick up his toys that typically end up all over the house, making wheelchair mobility difficult. It also happened when were out walking trails and he needed to drag a branch over to the side so I could easily pass.

Emotionally Moses helps me as well. He helps me meet new people, he makes me feel like I always have a loyal companion by my side, and he cheers me up if I get down and start to ask, why me?

Sometimes my wheelchair puts people off. They are not sure how to act, they worry they might say the wrong thing, or that they might reveal that they pity me. Moses' presence, however, takes all that away because the focus shifts from my chair to my dog. Further, most people can relate to a dog and are eager to share their stories about dogs in their life, so we can quickly find some common ground.

Once in a while, like most people I do get down and ask why me, but I don't ask that for long because I know that if I had not ended up in a wheelchair, I never would have had the great gift of Moses! He is the silver lining in my situation and hardly a day goes by that I do not feel tremendous gratitude for Moses and the people behind Canine Companions for Independence.

Lastly, I want to add that Moses helps me on a spiritual level. This is the hardest to explain, but I will give it a try with an example. Moses and I regularly go to the Spa State Park for long walks. I turn my wheelchair speed up as fast as it goes so Moses can trot or lope beside me. When we get away from the other walkers I look down at him. His ears are flopping, his mouth is slightly open, his tongue hangs to one side and he looks like he is smiling. As he breaks into a lope, he glances up at me and there is a magical moment when we are in sync and perfect harmony. We are connected in a beautiful and powerful human/ dog partnership.

To close my talk at the church service I stated metaphorically, "Moses diminishes [parts] the impediments [the red sea] that prevent me [the enslaved Israelites] from moving forward to regain my independence [reach the promised land]!

---

## A Two-Week Road Trip (From a Lab's Point of View)
(Nov. 11, 2011)

I knew something was going on when I saw Jill, my human companion and her husband, Steve bring out the suitcases. Jill had a list and checked it off as they packed clothes and other things. Next, they started loading up the car. When I saw them carry out a big bag of my dog food and put it into the car, I knew I was going to be part of whatever was happening. I should not have worried about being left behind since Jill takes me everywhere she goes, even once or twice on an airplane. Soon a nice lady came by to meet the cats, Sully and Magic. If I understood correctly this lady was a cat sitter who was going to come feed them and even play with them every evening while we were gone. I assured my feline friends everything was going to be fine because they were going to be in good hands. As we drove off I heard Jill and Steve say they would miss the cats, but how they really needed to get away for a time. They talked about how they had no plans except to have a good time together. So off we went for a real adventure with no definite plans.

Because I am a proud certified service dog that graduated from the Canine Companions For Independence Training Center on Long Island, I can go anywhere Jill goes when I wear my official vest and Jill carries my license. This is a freedom guaranteed by federal legislation known as the Americans with Disabilities Act. Nevertheless, to my surprise once we were on the road we ran into some hassles over my presence. Apparently some hotel managers have never heard of the law! When questions arose about me, I felt indignant, but Jill kept her cool and simply showed them a page from her AAA guide that explains the law. It even shows a picture of a man in a wheelchair with a lab like me sitting next to him in front of a hotel clerk. Not only must they accept me, they cannot add an extra charge as they can for pets. Some of the hotels charge an extra $50 or more for a pet. This is something to take into consideration if you plan on traveling with your pet.

Our journey took us to Pennsylvania, Maryland, West Virginia, Virginia, Kentucky, and Ohio. Jill said I was a great "ice-breaker" because everywhere we went people would come up and ask about me. This happens at home, but out in some of these areas people start by saying, "You got a nice D-A-W-W-G there." For some reason "dog" becomes "Dawwg" the further south you go. Everyone in the South also seemed really nice and polite too. Maybe that is why when Jill and Steve were eating lunch at a truck stop diner, the whole place went silent when Steve mentioned to a trucker we were from New York. Maybe they think New Yorkers are rude or too liberal or somehow strange.

Along the way we stopped at historic places like Gettysburg, Harper's Ferry, and too many museums. They might be interesting places for Jill and Steve, but for me they are just very slow walks with Jill as she reads all the signage and gradually moves on to the next glass case. No, museums are not for me, but what I loved was walking with Jill along rural roads and sniffing all kinds of new smells. In Pennsylvania, we saw lots of little farms and farm animals. In the Amish country we even saw horse-drawn buggies. The Amish farms were beautiful, but I had to wonder about the stories I have heard about the Amish running puppy mills. I hope that is not true because puppy mills are inhumane. Some poor dogs live in tiny cages where they must breed until they drop and then they are discarded because they are no longer of any use. If you are looking for a puppy always go a shelter or a reputable breeder. Puppies for sale in pet shops are almost always from puppy mills. So I figure that if people stop buying puppies from pet stores, the puppy mills will no longer have a market for their trade and eventually puppy mills will be a thing of the past.

There was one place with museums that I did enjoy. It was the Kentucky Horse Park and the International Museum of the Horse. I think it is pretty cool that there is such a grand place in honor of the horse. I wonder if there is such a place in honor of the dog? After all, it seems to me horses are just extra big dogs. Right? Anyway, the people there liked that we came from Saratoga Springs and they knew all about our horse track.

Between stops, I usually slept on the back seat as we drove through fields, mountains, towns, and cities. Jill and Steve were careful to stop frequently for me to stretch, relieve myself, and drink some fresh water. Also, because they were eating out most meals and Jill rarely cleans her plate, she would wrap up her scraps and let me have them during the day. At home I never get any people food, but on this trip I got to have a few bites of steak, chicken, liver, and pizza! I even got to have a few shrimp. At first I didn't know what they were so I ate one, tail and all. Then Steve taught me to take the shrimp between my teeth and gently pull it from his hand so the tail stayed behind. I learn fast especially when it comes to something tasty. Nevertheless, Jill reminded me not to get used to people food because at home we would go back to the old rules—kibble, kibble, and more boring, but healthy kibble.

My word, I have been rambling on and I didn't even get to the best parts of the trip. That is, I came face to face with the big buck behind one of our hotels and I got to visit two really fun dog parks. I guess I will write about those parts of the trip next week. Oh yes, I almost forgot to mention I turned four years old during the trip!

## The Road Trip, Part II
(Nov. 18, 2011)

Last week Jill let me tell about our two-week road trip, but I ran out of space before I got to describe what I considered the best parts of the trip—the dog parks and my encounter with a six-point buck.

Saratoga Springs is said to be a very dog-friendly town, and in many ways it is but there are no real dog parks. Yes, I know about the area over by Crescent Street and Route

9, but because it is not fenced, Jill doesn't think it is safe so she won't take me there. Nevertheless, she loves the idea of a safe dog park so on the trip we visited two and boy was it fun.

The first one we went to was in Fallston, Maryland. It took us several hours to get there and by the time we found it, it was closed! I was really disappointed but Jill said we would stay in a motel nearby and come back in the morning. So the next morning we returned to Rebel's Dog Park. It was fenced with a double-gated entry, benches, shade, water, and a separate area for small dogs. It was early so there were only two other dogs for me to run with, but they were both fun. One was a female German Shepherd and the other was a male Blue Tick Hound. With my leash off I could run and run at top speed. We only stopped to play tug of war with an old torn basketball or to gulp down some water. While we played Jill and Steve talked with the two other handlers. Once or twice they would call to us dogs if we were getting too carried away, but that only happened a couple of times. After about an hour and a half, I was ready to drop and Jill and Steve were ready to move on.

The second dog park we visited was in northern Kentucky. This one was named the Kenton County Kentucky Paw Park. It was just outside of Covington, situated by a beautiful creek, trees, and grassy picnic area. The Paw Park was larger than the Rebel's Park, but it still was fenced with a double-gated entry. We arrived in the mid-afternoon and there were lots of dogs. Again there was a separate area for small dogs and one for big dogs. The big dog area was about two acres in size and at one point there were twenty–five big dogs all running and playing. As some dogs left others came and there was always a greeting ritual when a new dog entered. The handlers sat on benches or stood watching as the dogs formed and reformed groups for games of chase. There was one small terrier-type dog that by size should have been with the smaller dogs, but he could run so fast it made all us big dogs look clumsy and slow. Even dogs with big strides couldn't keep up with this terrier that ran circles around all of us. There was plenty of fresh water and doggie poop bags for handlers to clean up after their dog.

I slept great that night. As I was drifting off I thought about the dog parks and how much fun I had running free off my leash. I also thought about what Jill said it would take to get a safe fenced dog park established around Saratoga.

These dog parks were a blast, but for me the most exciting moment of the entire trip occurred on the second to the last night before we arrived home. We were staying in a motel in Pickerington, Ohio. After Jill fed me my dinner, she took me behind the place so I could "do my business." After she cleaned it up as she always does with a doggy poop bag, we noticed a swamp beyond the parking lot with a sign that read, "Do not feed the wildlife." I wanted to get into the swamp for a dip, but it was dusk and Jill was ready to call it a day so we went back to the room.

Later that night after Jill fell asleep, Steve took me out one last time. I was sniffing for the perfect spot to relieve myself, when I looked up and saw him. He was a six-point buck about 20 yards away from me. He made a coughing, grunting noise and there was a doe behind him. They both stared at us. I froze in my tracks. I didn't know what to do, but every nerve in my body was tense and ready for action. I was so excited I quivered all over. After what seemed like five minutes, but was probably a few seconds, the buck and doe turned and vanished into the dark. This was the first buck I have ever seen. It wasn't a horse or a dog, but it was something else entirely. I'll never forget his majesty, his smell, his grunt, and the steam coming from his nostrils.

## The Holidays And A New Family Pet
(Dec. 16, 2011)

Are you considering a new pet to join your family this holiday season? If so, are you thinking about a dog, cat, parakeet, hamster, lizard, or a tank of tropical fish? These are all wonderful ideas for making the holidays memorable and exciting for you and your children. Nevertheless, there are some things to consider before making your purchase.

First of all you need to ask yourself, what kind of pet is best for your family at this time? Do any of the children have allergies to pet dander? If the answer is yes, a dog or cat is not the best idea. Who will be responsible for feeding and exercising the animal? If your children are too young or too busy with activities to take on this responsibility, do you have the time in your full schedule? If the answer is no, then pets requiring lower maintenance, like a bird or fish or a lizard may be the best choice. Even these pets, however, need some time and attention. And finally, can you afford the costs of care for the new pet? What equipment is necessary, what kinds of vet bills should you expect, and what will be the feeding costs? If you have honestly considered the issues of cost, time, and compatibility, you are ready to make an informed decision about a pet for your family.

The holidays may at first seem like the perfect time to surprise everyone with a new pet, but there are some issues to consider. The new animal may become overwhelmed with all the holiday excitement and activity. Children running through the house with their squeals of delight could be terrifying for a new kitten or even an adult cat. One option to consider is to wrap and present the equipment needed for the animal, to be opened on the holiday itself, and if the promise is for a dog or a fancy breed cat, take a family trip to the Saratoga County Animal Shelter or another "rescue only" venue the following day or week to find the actual pet.

Notice that I do not recommend a regular pet store if you are looking for a dog or a special breed cat because they perpetuate the horrific puppy mill industry. Puppy mills are places where breeding animals are kept in tiny cages for the sole purpose of constant reproduction, until they can breed no more and are simply discarded. It is an inhumane situation and the pet stores that buy and sell the puppies and kittens just perpetuate the system. To avoid being on the consumer end of this terrible trade, do not buy dogs or cats on the Internet or from classified ads listing several litters of several different breeds. Instead look for your new family pet at a local animal shelter, rescue group, or a pet store that deals only in rescued animals, making their store profits only on pet supplies.

Since the 1960s the federal government has regulated puppy mills, but the standards they set are little more than requiring food, water, and shelter. It is perfectly legal for licensed breeders to own 1,000 dogs or more; to keep all their dogs in wire cages for their entire lives with no more than six inches of space on all sides of the animal; and to breed animals as often as possible. Furthermore, there are too few inspectors to patrol the thousands of licensed breeders and kennels.

Rather than support puppy mills, choose to rescue and give a loving puppy, kitten, dog or cat a second chance. Up to 25% of dogs in shelters are purebreds, so even if you have your heart set on a particular breed, the best choice is adoption from a shelter or a specific breed rescue organization. Four to five million dogs are euthanized every year in our country—roughly 11,000 animals every single day! Make a difference and adopt.

## Jessie Finds Her Forever Home
(Jan. 13, 2012)

I frequently urge people to adopt their next pet from the county shelter. There are so many animals waiting there for a forever home. People need to realize, however, that some of these homeless creatures come with "baggage" from their earlier life experiences. Sometimes the animal's history has not been positive and as a result will present challenges for the new adopting family. Nevertheless, working with these homeless pets can be very rewarding. In fact, each animal we have brought into our home has taught us something important about animal behavior, training, and trust, as well as something about ourselves.

Last fall my husband Steve and I decided it was time to adopt a second dog. We typically enjoy having two dogs and it had been over a year since my first service dog, Vida passed "over the rainbow bridge," leaving Moses as the only dog in our household along with our two cats. It is not a good idea to adopt a new pet immediately after the passing of your beloved former pet because you have not had time to grieve and you may become impatient with the new one because it is not at all like the one you so desperately wish was still by your side.

While I am a lab lover, Steve has always had a soft spot for shepherds so we started looking at the Saratoga County Animal Shelter for a shepherd-type dog that needed a home. After a few weeks, we saw a photo on the shelter web page of a stray dog the employees had named Jessie. She looked like a beautiful black or very dark brown Belgian Shepherd mix. I drove over to see her. She was on the small side, but very alert, and curious about me. I sat with her for a time and learned what I could about her story.

Jessie had been picked up as a stray in Milton. She had on a yellow collar, but no tags. No one came looking for her.

No one called about her. I couldn't help wonder why no one was searching for this fine-looking girl. Her teeth indicated that she was around two years old. She had been spayed and she appeared to be in good health.

Next I brought Moses to meet Jessie. With supervision by the shelter employee who was working with Jessie, we watched the two dogs play in an open area. They seemed to be getting along well. Finally Steve came out to meet her. After another day to think about it, Steve was ready to adopt Jessie.

After bringing her home we quickly learned that she was very affectionate, knew basic commands, and was full of energy. We also learned that like most herding dogs she had a "high prey drive." In other words, she would chase anything that ran from her. In our fenced backyard this meant she chased squirrels, but in the house she chased the cats. Our very social male tiger cat, Sully loved the game, but our more reclusive female black cat, Magic was not amused at all. We also learned that Jessie displayed fear aggression whenever a stranger approached her. She would bark, bare her teeth, and look like she could rip out the stranger's throat! This time it was our vet that was not amused.

With Moses Jessie always wanted to play rough. At first Moses would wrestle with her and he always won due to his greater size. Nevertheless, Jessie always wanted more and after a few weeks, Moses, whose inclination is to be a lover, not a fighter grew tired of Jessie's constant attempts to engage him in rough and tumble play. When they were both outside in the yard Jessie would try to herd Moses by running at him, nipping his hindquarters and barking. If we were raising sheep all these behaviors would be very useful, but poor Moses would look up at me as if to ask, "Why did you bring her home? Can't we trade her in for another kind of dog?" Unfortunately, many people do return an adopted dog at the first sign of problems rather than allowing time for the animal and the family to adjust. Besides Steve was already very attached to Jessie and her shepherd ways.

Unlike Steve, I was not so happy about Jessie. Next to Moses she seemed much too busy all the time. One day I wanted to see if I could tire her out so I took her for a five-mile trot alongside my wheelchair at top speed. After our run I brought her home and she bolted out into the yard with reserve energy to chase a few squirrels! Was there no limit to this dog's energy?

To deal with her fear aggression upon meeting new people, we resorted to putting her outside until our guests were in the living room sitting comfortably in chairs. If they wanted to meet Jessie, we told them we would be letting Jessie in, but they had to act as if she was invisible (no eye contact, no touch, no talk) until she greeted them and she had their scent. This worked beautifully. When she can make the first move, she is not afraid and only wants to make friends. If people do not want to go along with this, we just let her stay outside with her squirrel duty. After all, she is the type of dog that needs a job.

We have now had Jessie in our home for almost three months and she has already calmed down considerably. She and the cats have worked things out in their own ways. Steve has taken her through six weeks of obedience training, and I have stopped unfairly comparing her to Moses who is a very different breed and who had two years of professional training to be a service dog. Actually, I have begun to appreciate Jessie for Jessie. Like all the other pets we have had over the years she is teaching me something about acceptance, patience, and maybe even love. Happy New Year!

## Closing

Moses and I want to thank everyone for purchasing our book and reading our stories. Even Jessie, Sully, and Magic say thanks. We all appreciate that by purchasing this book you have helped our homeless friends waiting patiently at the Saratoga County Animal Shelter, Estherville, or with H.O.P.E. We urge you all to continue looking out for lost, neglected or abused pets. They need your concern and your voice. We count on you to teach your children about loving and caring for animals. We also wish you many wonderful times ahead with your pets, walking together, playing together, and just sitting, resting, and dreaming together. It can be a most beautiful inter-species partnership.